THE ULTIMATE
ATLANTA FALCONS
TRIVIA BOOK

A Collection of Amazing Trivia Quizzes
and Fun Facts for Die-Hard Falcons Fans!

Ray Walker

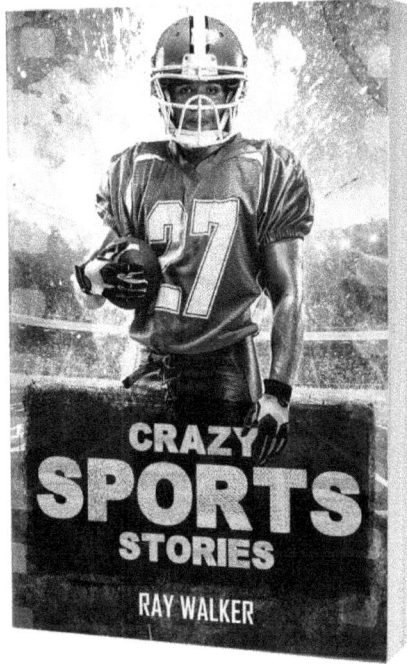

CONTENTS

INTRODUCTION

There is no sugarcoating it: The Atlanta Falcons have had a rough history since entering the National Football League. There have been some highs, including a pair of Super Bowl appearances, but there have also been plenty of lows along the way. No one is going to forget the 28-3 lead that vanished against the Patriots or the missed chances at greatness along the way. So many of the league's most exciting players have made their way through Atlanta, but the Falcons are still searching for that first Super Bowl championship. Through it all, the Atlanta fan base has stayed loyal to the Falcons, and fans are anticipating the success the franchise will have in the near future.

This trivia book is going to cover the entire history of the Atlanta Falcons from opening day at Atlanta-Fulton County Stadium through the end of the 2020 season. We are going to talk about all of the highs, some of the lows, and everything in between throughout the 12 chapters in this book. Each chapter contains plenty of fun facts and interesting nuggets with the common goal of making you a more knowledgeable fan of the Atlanta Falcons at the end of it. If we're successful, you will know far more about the Falcons than when you first took this book off the shelf.

The questions in this book are designed to be a little bit difficult to keep you hanging on the edge of your seat as you engage with the facts. Each of the 12 chapters focuses on a specific topic from the history of the program to specific positions and even the record book. In each chapter, there are 20 multiple-choice or true-false questions, followed by the answers to those questions on a separate page, and then 10 interesting tidbits about that chapter's topic that will hopefully give you some behind-the-scenes information. So please do not be alarmed if some of these questions stump you; the whole point of the book is to help you learn more about your favorite team, so don't expect to ace every chapter.

We want you to learn something new by devouring this book so that you can use your newfound knowledge to show off to your fellow fans. All of the information in this book is current as of the end of the 2020 season, so be warned that you might know more about the future by the time you pick up this book. All you need to do now is sit back, relax, and enjoy the hours of fun this book provides for the biggest Atlanta Falcons fans in the world.

CHAPTER 1:

ORIGINS & HISTORY

QUIZ TIME!

1. In June of which year did the NFL officially award a franchise to Atlanta?

    a. 1968

    b. 1967

    c. 1966

    d. 1965

2. What business was Rankin Smith in before he purchased the rights to the Falcons franchise?

    a. Life insurance

    b. Soft drinks

    c. Cable news

    d. Hardware

3. How quickly did the Falcons sell out their allotment of 45,000 season tickets?

    a. 48 days

    b. 51 days

c. 54 days

d. 57 days

4. Who was the first head coach in Falcons history?

   a. Vince Dooley

   b. Phil Bengtson

   c. Norb Hecker

   d. Norm Van Brocklin

5. The Falcons lost every preseason game in their first season in 1966.

   a. True

   b. False

6. After losing their first nine regular-season games, which team did Atlanta defeat for its first win as a franchise?

   a. St. Louis Rams

   b. New York Giants

   c. Minnesota Vikings

   d. Dallas Cowboys

7. When did the Falcons win their first division title?

   a. 1969

   b. 1973

   c. 1978

   d. 1980

8. The Falcons won the first playoff game they ever played.

   a. True

   b. False

9. Which non-interim head coach had the shortest tenure with the Falcons?

    a. Dan Henning
    b. Bobby Petrino
    c. June Jones
    d. Pat Peppler

10. Who is the winningest coach in Falcons history?

    a. Leeman Bennett
    b. Dan Reeves
    c. Mike Smith
    d. Norm Van Brocklin

11. Before it was known as the Stadium Authority, what was the name of the company Rankin Smith helped found to bring professional sports to Atlanta and build Atlanta-Fulton County Stadium?

    a. Georgians for Pro Sports
    b. Atlanta Premier Sports
    c. Major Sports, Inc.
    d. Rankin Smith Sports, Inc.

12. The Atlanta Falcons were one of the two teams to play in the first football game in Atlanta-Fulton County Stadium.

    a. True
    b. False

13. Which team did the Falcons play in 1991 in their final game at Atlanta-Fulton County Stadium?

a. Los Angeles Rams
b. Seattle Seahawks
c. New Orleans Saints
d. Tampa Bay Buccaneers

14. Which team did Atlanta beat in its first game in the new Mercedes Benz Stadium in 2017?

a. Carolina Panthers
b. New Orleans Saints
c. Tampa Bay Buccaneers
d. Green Bay Packers

15. The Falcons won more games at the Georgia Dome than it lost at Atlanta-Fulton County Stadium.

a. True
b. False

16. How many times has Atlanta won its division?

a. 7
b. 6
c. 8
d. 5

17. In which season did the Falcons set their franchise record for fewest wins in a season?

a. 1969
b. 1968
c. 1967
d. 1966

18. Who was the first team Atlanta defeated in a playoff game?

    a. Dallas Cowboys
    b. Seattle Seahawks
    c. New York Giants
    d. Philadelphia Eagles

19. Who caught the first touchdown pass in Falcons history, which were also the first points in team history?

    a. Gary Barnes
    b. Junior Coffey
    c. Charlie Scales
    d. Ernie Wheelwright

20. In which year did Arthur Blank purchase the Falcons from the Smith family?

    a. 1999
    b. 2000
    c. 2001
    d. 2002

QUIZ ANSWERS

1. D – 1965

2. A – Life insurance

3. C – 54 days

4. C – Norb Hecker

5. B – False

6. B – New York Giants

7. D – 1980

8. A – True

9. B – Bobby Petrino

10. C – Mike Smith

11. C – Major Sports, Inc.

12. B – False

13. B – Seattle Seahawks

14. D – Green Bay Packers

15. A – True

16. A – 7

17. C – 1967

18. D – Philadelphia Eagles

19. A – Gary Barnes

20. D – 2002

DID YOU KNOW?

1. There was an intense war between the National Football League and the American Football League over the rights to put a pro football team in Atlanta. The Denver Broncos almost moved to the city before a last-second ownership change kept the Broncos in the Mile High City, but after that incident, the AFL committed to an Atlanta franchise that would be owned by the Cox Corporation. However, NFL commissioner Pete Rozelle was in secret talks with the Stadium Authority about awarding an NFL franchise to the city. The two leagues kept in talks with Atlanta about a professional football team before the NFL won out with Rankin Smith paying $8.5 million for the rights to the expansion franchise.

2. After being awarded the new franchise, Rankin Smith announced a contest to name Atlanta's new football team. Though several people submitted the name "Falcons," the winner was declared to be Julia Elliott, a teacher from Griffin, Georgia. In her submission, she said she chose the name because "the falcon is proud and dignified, with great courage and fight. It never drops prey. It is deadly and has a great sporting tradition."

3. The Falcons quickly set a record for ticket sales for a new franchise when they sold 45,000 season tickets in just 54 days after they went on sale to the public. When Rankin

Smith returned to his office at Life of Georgia Insurance from the introductory press conference, he had received more than 1,000 phone calls for tickets, and he received thousands of letters as well.

4. When searching for the team's first coach, Rankin Smith initially shot for the stars by talking with legendary Packers coach Vince Lombardi. When the coach turned down Smith's offers, the Falcons owner asked Lombardi for some recommendations. One name Lombardi did not mention was that of defensive assistant Norb Hecker. Smith thought Lombardi purposefully passed over Hecker's name to keep a talented assistant in Green Bay, so he decided to hire Hecker. After a 4-26-1 record, Hecker was fired and is still considered among the worst hires in franchise history.

5. The Falcons lost their first nine games before traveling to Yankee Stadium on November 20, 1966, to face the New York Giants. Ernie Wheelwright caught two touchdown passes from Randy Johnson sandwiched around a Johnson scoring pass to Vern Burke to build the lead, then Johnson sealed the game with a three-yard touchdown run to cap off a 27-16 win for the Falcons. Atlanta went on to win three of its final five games, including its first home win on December 11, a 16-10 victory over the Cardinals.

6. In 1978, the Falcons became one of the first teams to have a year-round practice facility when they opened theirs in Suwanee, Georgia. One of the most visible signs of the complex was the Falcon Inn, an old Ramada motel that

Rankin Smith bought and transformed into dorms for the Falcons during training camp, which also housed some of the players during the season. The building was torn down in 2007 after the team moved its training camp from Suwanee to Greenville, South Carolina, in 1999 and eventually moved into a new headquarters in Flowery Branch, Georgia, in 2004.

7. The Falcons' first foray into the postseason in 1978 featured a pair of dramatic fourth-quarter comebacks against current members of the NFC East. In the wild-card round, the Falcons entered the fourth quarter trailing Philadelphia 13-0, but Steve Bartkowski threw two touchdown passes in the final eight minutes of regulation to lift Atlanta to its first every playoff win. The following week, the Falcons traveled to Dallas and had the Cowboys on the ropes with a 20-13 lead at halftime. However, Dallas tied the game in the third quarter, then took the lead for good in the fourth quarter on the way to the Super Bowl.

8. The Georgia Dome was the product of Rankin Smith's overtly political tactics of hinting that he might move the Falcons to Jacksonville, Florida, in the late 1980s. Though there were never serious discussions with the city of Jacksonville, it got the ball rolling on a deal after five years of conversations about financing a new stadium. In January 1989, the team and the state agreed to a 20-year lease for the Georgia Dome and construction began the following year. The Falcons moved into the new stadium

in 1992, and the dome hosted Super Bowl XXVIII and Super Bowl XXXIV. The Falcons finished with a 116-83-0 regular-season record in the Georgia Dome, nearly reversing their 84-106-2 record at Atlanta-Fulton County Stadium.

9. After Rankin Smith's death in 1997, there were several rumors about the Smith family potentially selling the Falcons. Team president Taylor Smith shot down the stories each time, but by the end of 2001, there appeared to be a deal imminent between the Smith children and Home Depot founder Arthur Blank. Blank had spoken with Rankin Smith 15 years before to discuss buying the team, but there was no interest at that time. In November 2001, Blank reportedly offered Taylor Smith $500 million for the franchise, and Smith publicly said the team was not for sale. However, when Blank upped the offer by roughly 10%, it was harder for the Smith family to ignore. The deal was agreed upon in December, and, the day before Super Bowl XXXVI in February 2002, the league approved Blank's purchase, and he assumed control of the franchise.

10. The Falcons have made the playoffs 14 times in their history and have won their division six times. Atlanta has a 369-473-6 record in regular-season games with a 215-208-2 record at home and a 154-265-4 record on the road.

CHAPTER 2:

NUMBERS GAME

QUIZ TIME!

1. The Falcons have had a player wear every number between 1 and 99.

   a. True
   b. False

2. Which was the last single-digit number to be worn by a Falcons player?

   a. 9
   b. 6
   c. 5
   d. 2

3. Who was the first Falcons player to wear number 7 after Michael Vick's exit from the team?

   a. No one
   b. Shayne Graham
   c. Byron Leftwich
   d. Younghoe Koo

4. Which backup quarterback wore number 8 between Matt Schaub's two stints with the Falcons?

   a. Matt Simms
   b. Chris Redman
   c. Joey Harrington
   d. Sean Renfree

5. Atlanta's first starting quarterback, Randy Johnson, shared a uniform number with which current Falcons player?

   a. Calvin Ridley
   b. Christian Blake
   c. Julio Jones
   d. Sterling Hofrichter

6. Who is the only player to wear number 10 after Steve Bartkowski's departure from Atlanta in 1985?

   a. Ty Detmer
   b. Doug Johnson
   c. Chris Chandler
   d. Scott Campbell

7. Which of these players also wore number 21, which Deion Sanders made famous in Atlanta?

   a. Allen Rossum
   b. Gerald McBurrows
   c. DeAngelo Hall
   d. Dunta Robinson

8. Which number was Jamal Anderson wearing when he bulldozed his way through defenses for the Falcons?

a. 34

b. 33

c. 32

d. 30

9. William Andrews is the last player to wear number 31 for the Falcons.

   a. True

   b. False

10. Which of these players did NOT wear number 42 after Gerald Riggs left Atlanta?

    a. Patrick DiMarco

    b. T.J. Duckett

    c. Jamal Robertson

    d. Sean Boyd

11. What number did Jessie Tuggle wear while roaming sideline to sideline for the Falcons in the 1990s?

    a. 54

    b. 56

    c. 58

    d. 59

12. Which number did Alge Crumpler wear for the Falcons during his seven-year stay in Atlanta?

    a. 83

    b. 85

    c. 87

    d. 88

13. The Falcons have players wearing every number in the 90s on their roster.

    a. True

    b. False

14. Which of these Ring of Honor honorees was NOT the first player to wear his number?

    a. Gerald Riggs

    b. Mike Kenn

    c. Claude Humphrey

    d. Jeff Van Note

15. Which of these players has NOT had his number honored in the Atlanta Falcons Ring of Honor?

    a. Jamal Anderson

    b. Warrick Dunn

    c. Roddy White

    d. Deion Sanders

16. Officially, the Falcons do not retire numbers, but, unofficially, certain numbers will never be worn again, like which number that Atlanta honored for Tommy Nobis?

    a. 58

    b. 60

    c. 63

    d. 68

17. What color was the original Falcons helmet worn in the inaugural 1966 season?

a. Black

b. Red

c. White

d. Blue

18. In which year did the Falcons first introduce a red jersey into their uniform collection?

    a. 1971

    b. 1980

    c. 1992

    d. 2003

19. In which year did the Falcons introduce a black helmet?

    a. 1966

    b. 1971

    c. 1983

    d. 1990

20. What is written in capital letters across the new uniforms that the Falcons introduced for the 2020 season?

    a. PEACH CITY

    b. FALCONS

    c. ATLANTA

    d. ATL

QUIZ ANSWERS

1. A – True

2. D – 2

3. D – Younghoe Koo

4. B – Chris Redman

5. C – Julio Jones

6. D – Scott Campbell

7. C – DeAngelo Hall

8. C – 32

9. A – True

10. B – T.J. Duckett

11. C – 58

12. A – 83

13. B – False

14. C – Claude Humphrey

15. A – Jamal Anderson

16. B – 60

17. B – Red

18. A – 1971

19. D – 1990

20. D – ATL

DID YOU KNOW?

1. The Atlanta Falcons do not officially retire numbers, but they do have several numbers in the Ring of Honor, many of which have not been worn since they were honored. Atlanta has honored William Andrews (31), Steve Bartkowski (10), Warrick Dunn (28), Claude Humphrey (87), Mike Kenn (78), Tommy Nobis (60), Gerald Riggs (42), Deion Sanders (21), Jessie Tuggle (58), Jeff Van Note (57), and Roddy White (84).

2. Matt Ryan originally wanted to wear number 7 in high school because that was the number his uncle, John Loughery, wore during his football career. But that number wasn't available, so he decided on number 2 in honor of Tim Couch, who was on his way to being the 1st overall pick in the 1999 NFL Draft while playing at Kentucky while Ryan was in high school. He was also originally assigned number 12 when he enrolled at Boston College, but that was taken from him as well, so he switched back to number 2.

3. Ryan is by far the most successful Falcons player to wear number 2, but he also didn't have much competition for the honor. Clarence Verdin was the first player to wear the number, in 1994 as a returner for Atlanta. He set a career high by averaging 23.3 yards per kick return in his only year with the Falcons and also averaged 4.9 yards

per punt return. The only other player to have worn the number for Atlanta is Todd Peterson, in 2005 as the team's kicker. Peterson made 23 of his 25 field goal attempts with a long kick of 43 yards, and he converted all 35 extra points as well.

4. Sometimes it takes a little math trick to discover the true meaning behind certain jersey numbers. In Vic Beasley's case, he wore number 44 with the Falcons because he was the 8th overall pick and $4 + 4 = 8$. It's a similar situation with Mohammed Sanu, who chose his number 12 because he wore number 2 in high school and number 6 in college at Rutgers and $2 \times 6 = 12$.

5. Devonta Freeman honored his aunt by wearing number 24 for the Falcons during his tenure in Atlanta. Freeman's aunt died of a heart attack at the age of 24 in 2007 when Freeman was just 15 years old. He told the team website that the proximity in age made her one of his best friends in his family, so he wanted to find a way to honor her on the field. Freeman also said that his aunt was a big motivation for him to attend college and earn a degree because she was in college when she passed away.

6. The number 13 has not been lucky for the players who have worn the number during their time in Atlanta. Punter Chris Mohr wore the number the longest—four seasons from 2001 to 2004—and most of the others who have donned the jersey were quarterbacks. Billy Joe Tolliver wore the number in 1991, becoming the first Atlanta player

to choose the notoriously unlucky number, and he was followed in 1995 by Browning Nagle; Tony Graziani had the jersey in 1997 and 1998, then Danny Kannell wore number 13 in 1999 and 2000. Joey Harrington and T.J. Yates both also wore the number for Atlanta, but number 13 currently belongs to receiver Christian Blake.

7. When Younghoe Koo came onto the field on November 10, 2019, he became the first player to wear number 7 for the Falcons since Michael Vick left the team. He made all four of his field goals and kicked two extra points to be named the NFC Special Teams Player of the Week in his debut, but many fans were talking about his choice of number. He said he didn't ask for the number, and it was simply issued to him by the team, but Koo has certainly done number 7 justice in his time with the Falcons.

8. Deion Sanders warned Todd Gurley not to take his number 21 when Gurley signed with the Falcons before the 2020 season. However, the running back decided to don the number because number 30, the number he wore with the Rams, was unavailable in Atlanta. Gurley is the eighth player to wear number 21 since Sanders left Atlanta, joining other notable names like cornerbacks DeAngelo Hall and Desmond Trufant, who at least played the same position as Sanders. Hall said he specifically chose number 21 in honor of Sanders, whom he idolized growing up.

9. The Falcons didn't introduce a red jersey until 1971 when it became the color for the team's primary home uniform.

Red remained the team's home jersey until 1990 when the franchise returned to black for its home jerseys. A red jersey returned as an alternate jersey for two games in 2003 and then was promoted back to the primary home jersey in 2004. Red is an important color for the city of Atlanta because every major sports team and most of the iconic international brands based in Atlanta use red in some fashion. That history is a big reason why the Falcons' Color Rush uniforms are an all-red combination of jerseys, pants, and socks.

10. Atlanta began its franchise with red helmets and kept the color for the first 25 years of existence. In 1990, the Falcons introduced their black helmets and have kept that as their main helmet for the last 30 seasons.

CHAPTER 3:

CALLING THE SIGNALS

QUIZ TIME!

1. Matt Ryan is the runaway leader for most games as Atlanta's starting quarterback with how many starts for the Falcons?

   a. 198
   b. 201
   c. 205
   d. 209

2. Who was the Falcons' starting quarterback when the franchise won its first game in 1966?

   a. Bob Berry
   b. Randy Johnson
   c. Steve Sloan
   d. Dennis Claridge

3. Who was the first Atlanta quarterback to throw for 2,000 yards in a season?

a. Randy Johnson
b. Steve Bartkowski
c. Bob Lee
d. Bob Berry

4. Matt Ryan has twice as many passing yards, passing touchdowns, completions, and passing attempts in his Atlanta career as the player in second place in those categories.

a. True
b. False

5. Before Matt Ryan broke it three times, what was the Falcons' record for most passing touchdowns in a season?

a. 31
b. 30
c. 32
d. 29

6. How many rushing yards did Michael Vick have during his Falcons career, the seventh-most in franchise history?

a. 3,692
b. 3,859
c. 3,968
d. 4,012

7. How many passes did Chris Miller attempt in 1989 to set the Falcons' record for most passing attempts in a single game?

a. 59
b. 62

c. 66

d. 68

8. Matt Ryan is the only other quarterback in Falcons history with more than 700 rushing yards in their career.

   a. True
   b. False

9. Which quarterback replaced Michael Vick due to injury for most of the 2003 season?

   a. Kurt Kittner
   b. Chris Chandler
   c. Doug Johnson
   d. Matt Schaub

10. Who was the last quarterback NOT named Matt Ryan to win a game as Atlanta's starting quarterback?

    a. Byron Leftwich
    b. Joey Harrington
    c. Matt Schaub
    d. Chris Redman

11. Against which team did Steve Bartkowski become the first Falcons quarterback to throw for 400 yards in a game?

    a. Miami Dolphins
    b. Green Bay Packers
    c. New Orleans Saints
    d. Pittsburgh Steelers

12. In which year did Steve Bartkowski become the first Falcons quarterback to throw for 3,000 yards in a season?

a. 1979

b. 1980

c. 1981

d. 1982

13. The 1998 season was the only year in which Chris Chandler had a winning record as the Falcons' starting quarterback.

a. True

b. False

14. Chris Chandler was a two-time Pro Bowler with the Falcons. In which other year besides 1998 was Chandler named to the Pro Bowl?

a. 1996

b. 1997

c. 1999

d. 2000

15. What is Michael Vick's career high in rushing yards with Atlanta?

a. 151

b. 167

c. 173

d. 182

16. How many times did Michael Vick throw for 3,000 yards in a season for the Falcons?

a. 3

b. 2

c. 1

d. 0

17. Michael Vick holds the Falcons' record for consecutive games without throwing an interception.

a. True

b. False

18. Which Falcons passing record does Matt Ryan NOT hold?

a. Career interception percentage

b. Career passer rating

c. Passes completed in a game

d. Consecutive games with a touchdown pass

19. In which season was Matt Ryan named the NFL MVP?

a. 2017

b. 2015

c. 2018

d. 2016

20. Matt Ryan's franchise record for completion percentage in a season is above 70%.

a. True

b. False

QUIZ ANSWERS

1. C – 205

2. B – Randy Johnson

3. D – Bob Berry

4. A – True

5. A – 31

6. B – 3,859

7. C – 66

8. A – True

9. C – Doug Johnson

10. D – Chris Redman

11. D – Pittsburgh Steelers

12. B – 1980

13. A – True

14. B – 1997

15. C – 173

16. D – 0

17. A – True

18. C – Passes completed in a game

19. D – 2016

20. B – False

DID YOU KNOW?

1. Atlanta's first quarterback was Randy Johnson, who was chosen with the second of their 1st round picks in the 1966 Draft. He was battered while playing behind the offensive line of an expansion franchise and won just eight games for the Falcons before they traded him to the Giants. However, his story had a sad ending; after he divorced his wife once his playing career ended, Johnson fell into a deep depression and turned to drinking to cope with the loneliness. He eventually died from the effects of alcoholism in 2012 at the age of 65.

2. Bob Berry's first start in the NFL came in 1966 against the Atlanta Falcons, a game Atlanta won 20-13. The Minnesota coach who gave Berry that start was Norm Van Brocklin, and the pair reunited in Atlanta in 1968. Under Van Brocklin's tutelage in Atlanta, Berry completed 57% of his passes, throwing 57 touchdowns and 56 interceptions in 50 starts for the Falcons.

3. Steve Bartkowski had a troubled life for the first three years after Atlanta drafted him 1st overall in 1975. Bartkowski had grown up idolizing Joe Namath, so he tried to emulate him as much as he could on and off the field. However, once he was a starting quarterback in the NFL, Bartkowski said he realized how empty his life felt trying to be Joe Namath. It all came to a head in 1978

when the Falcons started June Jones in a preseason game instead of Bartkowski, and the quarterback admitted that he didn't want to deal with anyone. After the game, Bartkowski vowed to change himself for the better; the wild stories about him ceased, and he found a much happier and successful career ahead of him.

4. Chris Miller made an instant impression the first time he took the field as the Falcons' quarterback in 1987. The brash rookie had held out until the end of October, so he didn't make his debut for Atlanta until December, with the Falcons en route to another forgettable season. But, in that huddle, Miller told veteran offensive linemen Bill Fralic and Mike Kenn to shut up because he was running the team now. The results didn't pan out immediately, but in 1988, Miller's presence made a huge difference for the Falcons. Atlanta scored 10 more points and gained 40 more yards per game on average with Miller in the lineup than without him.

5. June Jones's decision to bench Jeff George in a 1996 blowout spiraled into the end of George's career in Atlanta. George followed Jones down the sideline, berating him for the decision, and the Falcons suspended him for conduct detrimental to the team. A month later, Atlanta released George because no suitable trade partners were willing to take on George's salary. The closest was a reported trade with Seattle, with the Seahawks offering George a restructured contract, but George decided against signing the deal because he felt rushed into making a decision.

6. Chris Chandler's career was saved in 1991 by a quarterbacks coach in Arizona. Jerry Rhome saw an angry young quarterback who was mad at the world and told him that he would help him if he dropped his attitude. Chandler had his reasons to be angry after his mother died when he was 19, and his father passed away shortly after Chandler was drafted into the NFL. The constant moving from team to team didn't help him either, but Rhome was able to rekindle his passion for the game, and former 49ers quarterback John Brodie, Chandler's father-in-law, helped him regain the confidence he needed.

7. Michael Vick's story might be the biggest what-if in Atlanta sports history. Vick electrified Falcons fans with his athleticism for six years after being drafted 1st overall in the 2001 NFL Draft. But, shortly before the 2007 season was set to begin, Vick was suspended indefinitely for his role in an underground dogfighting ring in his native Virginia. Vick served 21 months in federal prison for the dogfighting charges, and the Falcons released him in 2009 after failing to find a suitable trade partner for Vick's rights.

8. Matt Schaub is probably best known for being a member of the Falcons despite only starting three games in seven combined seasons with the team. He lost all three of those starts but impressed many with his poise and talent in those appearances. In his second career start, Schaub threw for 298 yards and three touchdowns as he went toe-to-toe with Tom Brady in 2005. After being dealt to

Houston and having some success as a starter for various teams, Schaub returned to Atlanta to be Matt Ryan's backup. In his only start, Schaub threw for 460 yards—the second-most yardage in Falcons history—in a loss to the Seahawks in 2019.

9. Since the Falcons drafted Matt Ryan in 2008, no other quarterback has won a game for the Falcons. Matt Schaub lost his only start in that time frame, and Chris Redman lost two starts in 2009. But Redman also has the last win by an Atlanta quarterback who isn't Ryan. It came in the finale of the 2007 season against Seattle when he threw for 251 yards and four touchdowns in a 44-41 victory. Redman and Joey Harrington, who won three games in 2007, are the only other quarterbacks besides Michael Vick and Matt Ryan to win a game for the Falcons since 2004.

10. Matt Ryan is the only Falcons player to be named the NFL MVP, earning the honor in 2016. Ryan finished the year second in the NFL with 4,944 passing yards and 38 touchdown passes in leading the Falcons to the NFC South division title. Ryan only had six 300-yard passing games that season but did set the single-game record that year against the Panthers. Ryan's 69.9% completion percentage in 2016 still ranks as the franchise record and was third best in the league that year.

CHAPTER 4:

BETWEEN THE TACKLES

QUIZ TIME!

1. When did Dave Hampton become the first Falcons running back to rush for 1,000 yards in a season?

    a. 1976

    b. 1975

    c. 1973

    d. 1972

2. Who was the first Atlanta running back to rush for 200 yards in a game?

    a. Michael Turner

    b. Jamal Anderson

    c. Warrick Dunn

    d. Gerald Riggs

3. Whose record did Michael Turner tie when he ran for touchdowns in seven consecutive games in 2009?

    a. William Andrews

    b. Jamal Anderson

c. T.J. Duckett

d. Dave Hampton

4. Who holds the Falcons' record for the longest run from scrimmage with a 90-yard touchdown?

a. Warrick Dunn

b. Gerald Riggs

c. Michael Turner

d. Jerious Norwood

5. No Falcons player has led the team in rushing for five consecutive seasons.

a. True

b. False

6. Which of these running backs did NOT rush for 1,000 yards in three consecutive seasons?

a. Michael Turner

b. Gerald Riggs

c. Jamal Anderson

d. William Andrews

7. Who holds the Falcons' record for most 100-yard rushing games?

a. Jamal Anderson

b. Michael Turner

c. Warrick Dunn

d. Gerald Riggs

8. No Falcons running back has ever led the NFC in rushing.

a. True

b. False

9. Which Atlanta running back is the only Falcons player to ever lead the NFL in touchdowns when he shared the honor with 14 touchdowns?

a. William Andrews

b. Jamal Anderson

c. Devonta Freeman

d. T.J. Duckett

10. Who is the only Falcons running back with at least 150 carries to average five yards per carry for an entire season?

a. Warrick Dunn

b. Michael Turner

c. Jamal Anderson

d. Gerald Riggs

11. William Andrews set the franchise record for rushing yards in a game in his first NFL game.

a. True

b. False

12. How many yards per carry did William Andrews average over his career to set the Falcons' record?

a. 4.4

b. 4.5

c. 4.6

d. 4.7

13. In which season did Gerald Riggs set the Falcons' single-season rushing record before Jamal Anderson broke it in 1998?

    a. 1988
    b. 1987
    c. 1986
    d. 1985

14. Who was Atlanta playing when Gerald Riggs set his career high for rushing yards in a game in 1984?

    a. Houston Oilers
    b. Dallas Cowboys
    c. Kansas City Chiefs
    d. New Orleans Saints

15. Where does Jamal Anderson rank in Atlanta's record book for career rushing yards?

    a. 3rd
    b. 4th
    c. 5th
    d. 6th

16. What type of injury derailed Jamal Anderson's 1999 season after a career year in 1998?

    a. Concussion
    b. Turf toe
    c. Torn ACL
    d. Broken leg

17. How many times did Warrick Dunn rush for 10 touchdowns in a season for the Falcons?

    a. 3
    b. 2
    c. 1
    d. 0

18. Which was the only season Warrick Dunn was named to the Pro Bowl with the Falcons?

    a. 2005
    b. 2006
    c. 2007
    d. 2008

19. Michael Turner led the NFC in 2008 when he rushed for a career-best 1,699 yards in his first season with the Falcons.

    a. True
    b. False

20. How many rushing touchdowns did Michael Turner score in 2008 to set the Falcons' single-season record?

    a. 14
    b. 15
    c. 16
    d. 17

QUIZ ANSWERS

1. B – 1975

2. D – Gerald Riggs

3. C – T.J. Duckett

4. A – Warrick Dunn

5. B – False

6. A – Michael Turner

7. B – Michael Turner

8. B – False

9. C – Devonta Freeman

10. A – Warrick Dunn

11. A – True

12. C – 4.6

13. D – 1985

14. D – New Orleans Saints

15. C – 5th

16. C – Torn ACL

17. D – 0

18. A – 2005

19. B – False

20. D – 17

DID YOU KNOW?

1. Junior Coffey had never played any organized sports growing up as a black man in the small town of Dimmitt, Texas. Integration had not taken over the town in the 1950s, so Coffey was preparing for a life without sports at one of the few jobs black men could get in that part of the country. But two of his friends from school encouraged him to go out for the football team, and at 6 foot 1, 200 pounds, his natural athleticism shone through. He began as a defensive tackle on the high school team, but after he returned a fumble for a touchdown, the coaches put him at running back because they needed to find ways to get the ball in his hands.

2. One could argue that Dave Hampton was cursed while playing for the Falcons. The running back was poised to become the Falcons' first 1,000-yard rusher twice before he finally succeeded in 1975. In 1972, Hampton technically became the first Falcons player to hit the 1,000-yard mark on a one-yard rush that got him to 1,000 yards even, but he recovered a fumble in the fourth quarter for a six-yard loss and could not make up the lost yardage because Atlanta was trailing. The next year, the Falcons spent most of their season finale trying to get Hampton the 87 yards he needed for 1,000, but he fell three yards short, which was still technically closer than how he finished

1972. In 1975, Hampton looked destined to fall just shy of 1,000 yards again, but the Falcons sacrificed their chance at winning and gave Hampton the carries he needed to rush for 1,002 yards, then promptly removed him from the game.

3. William Andrews's mother didn't know he was playing football in middle school and at the beginning of high school. He had his brother forge his mom's signature, then took the sports section out of the local newspapers so she couldn't read about his accomplishments. The deception ended when a coach saw his mother at the grocery store and mentioned Andrews's exploits on the gridiron. She told him that he had to quit the team, so he went into his coach's office and relayed the message. Fortunately for Falcons fans, Andrews's coaches talked his mother into letting him play, and he went on to become one of the best running backs in Falcons history.

4. Gerald Riggs's football career was almost derailed before it began. Growing up in Las Vegas, Riggs found himself in trouble quite a bit, and his junior season was reduced to just three games because of disciplinary problems. However, his mother and stepfather helped him get back on the right track, and Riggs matured enough to play a full season his senior year at Bonanza High School and shine. He went on to have a successful career at Arizona State before being drafted by Atlanta in 1982.

5. Erric Pegram was a one-hit wonder for the Falcons in 1993 when he ran for 1,185 yards and three touchdowns. The 1991 draft pick led all the running backs in starts in his rookie season, but he never really dazzled anyone until the third game of the 1993 season. He ran the ball 27 times for 192 yards against San Francisco, one of his four 100-yard performances that season for the Falcons. He was unable to sustain that momentum in 1994 and ended up signing with Pittsburgh after that season.

6. Jamal Anderson will forever be known for his celebrated touchdown dance, "The Dirty Bird." The dance came about during a Falcons trip to play the Giants in Week 6 of that 1998 season, while the players were trying to drum up some interest in the team. The name derived from a comment a fan made after Atlanta demolished Carolina in Week 4 of the 1998 season, but the dance didn't debut until Week 7 when he scored against the Saints and started to flap his arms. The dance found its true form a few weeks later, and the dance craze swept Atlanta as the Falcons marched to the Super Bowl in 1998.

7. Atlanta's decision to draft T.J. Duckett in the 1st round of the 2002 Draft was very surprising to many Falcons fans. The team had just signed Warrick Dunn, and many had hoped that the Falcons would pair a number one receiver with new quarterback Michael Vick. Yet the decision worked out well for Atlanta, which finished second in the league in rushing in 2002, then led the league in rushing in 2004 en route to winning the NFC South crown. Duckett

was an integral part of that with his toughness around the goal line, scoring 31 times from 2002 to 2005, mostly in those short-yardage situations.

8. Warrick Dunn's love for the Atlanta Falcons extended off the field when he retired from the NFL after the 2008 season. The following year, Dunn reached an agreement to become a minority owner in the team, extending his reach in the Atlanta area. Throughout his career, Dunn was very active in the community, notably with his Homes for the Holidays initiative that has helped more than 90 single parents become first-time homeowners. In 2004, Dunn not only had his first of three straight 1,000-yard seasons for the Falcons but was also honored with the Walter Payton Man of the Year award for his service in the Atlanta community.

9. One of the best free-agent signings over the past two decades for the Falcons was Michael Turner, who was a seldom-used backup in San Diego. In his first game as a Falcons player, Turner set the single-game rushing record, and that 2008 season was his breakout campaign. He ran for 1,699 yards, the third most in franchise history, and he set the team record with 17 rushing touchdowns that year. He also led the NFL with 44 broken tackles, inviting contact and using his strength to plow for extra yards most backs couldn't obtain.

10. When he was just 11 years old, Devonta Freeman built a close bond with Luther Campbell, one of the founders of

the hip-hop group 2 Live Crew. Freeman grew up in the Liberal City housing projects in Miami, and it was there that he met Campbell, who helped steer Freeman toward his NFL career. Campbell would hire Freeman to do odd jobs around his house, helping the young Freeman earn money for his family in a more reputable way. The mentor-mentee relationship extended to Freeman's professional career because Campbell's wife served as Freeman's agent during his time with the Falcons.

CHAPTER 5:

CATCHING THE BALL

QUIZ TIME!

1. Who holds the Falcons' record for most consecutive games with a reception?

    a. Andre Rison

    b. Roddy White

    c. Julio Jones

    d. Alge Crumpler

2. Who was the first Falcons receiver with 1,000 receiving yards in a season?

    a. Alfred Jenkins

    b. Andre Rison

    c. Wallace Francis

    d. Stacey Bailey

3. Julio Jones and Roddy White are the only two receivers to have 200 or more receiving yards in a game.

    a. True

    b. False

4. Julio Jones and Roddy White are the clear top two in Falcons history for receptions, but who held the team record with 573 catches before the two arrived in Atlanta?

   a. Terance Mathis
   b. Alfred Jenkins
   c. Andre Rison
   d. William Andrews

5. Which of these Falcons receivers did NOT have at least ten 100-yard games for Atlanta?

   a. Terance Mathis
   b. Andre Rison
   c. Alfred Jenkins
   d. Harry Douglas

6. A wide receiver does NOT hold the Falcons' record for most catches in a game.

   a. True
   b. False

7. Who caught Bobby Hebert's 98-yard touchdown pass, the longest pass completion in Falcons history?

   a. Eric Metcalf
   b. Michael Haynes
   c. Bert Emanuel
   d. Andre Rison

8. Who is the Falcons' all-time leader in receiving yards by a tight end?

a. Alge Crumpler

b. Austin Hooper

c. Tony Gonzalez

d. Jim Mitchell

9. Who holds Atlanta's career record for receptions by a tight end?

a. Hayden Hurst

b. Jim Mitchell

c. Alge Crumpler

d. Tony Gonzalez

10. In which year did Alge Crumpler NOT lead the Falcons in receiving yards and receptions?

a. 2004

b. 2006

c. 2003

d. 2005

11. In which year did Alfred Jenkins become the first Falcons receiver to be named a First Team All-Pro by the Associated Press?

a. 1978

b. 1979

c. 1980

d. 1981

12. What is Andre Rison's franchise record for most touchdown catches in a season?

a. 13

b. 14

c. 15

d. 16

13. Terance Mathis was the first Atlanta player to have 100 catches in a season.

    a. True

    b. False

14. Terance Mathis holds the Falcons' record for most consecutive games with a receiving touchdown at how many games?

    a. 7

    b. 6

    c. 5

    d. 4

15. What is Roddy White's legal first name?

    a. Sharod

    b. Rodney

    c. Roderick

    d. Lamar

16. Roddy White still owns the Falcons' record for career touchdown receptions with how many?

    a. 57

    b. 59

    c. 61

    d. 63

17. Who was the only receiver to lead the Falcons in receiving yards between 2007 and 2019 NOT named Julio Jones or Roddy White?

    a. Tony Gonzalez

    b. Mohamed Sanu

    c. Harry Douglas

    d. Calvin Ridley

18. Julio Jones has had at least 1,000 yards in every season in which he's played at least 10 games.

    a. True

    b. False

19. In which year did Julio Jones set the Falcons' record for receiving yards and receptions in a single season?

    a. 2017

    b. 2016

    c. 2015

    d. 2014

20. What team were the Falcons playing when Julio Jones became the only wide receiver in franchise history to have 300 receiving yards in a game?

    a. Tampa Bay Buccaneers

    b. Carolina Panthers

    c. Dallas Cowboys

    d. New Orleans Saints

QUIZ ANSWERS

1. B – Roddy White

2. C – Wallace Francis

3. A – True

4. A – Terance Mathis

5. D – Harry Douglas

6. A – True

7. B – Michael Haynes

8. D – Jim Mitchell

9. D – Tony Gonzalez

10. C – 2003

11. D – 1981

12. C – 15

13. A – True

14. B – 6

15. A – Sharod

16. D – 63

17. C – Harry Douglas

18. B – False

19. C – 2015

20. B – Carolina Panthers

DID YOU KNOW?

1. The Falcons had their first great receiver playing in their backyard for four years and never realized it. Alfred Jenkins played college football at Morris Brown College in Atlanta but went undrafted in 17 rounds of the 1974 NFL Draft because he was only 5 foot 7. He ended up signing in the World Football League, where he had 60 catches for 1,326 yards and 12 touchdowns in his only season before the league folded. The Falcons saw the tape from the WFL and were impressed enough to sign Jenkins to a deal, and Atlanta found its first dominant receiver in franchise history.

2. Though Alge Crumpler and Tony Gonzalez deservedly garner the headlines as the best tight ends in Falcons history, both of them trail Jim Mitchell for most career receiving yards by a tight end. In 11 seasons in Atlanta, Mitchell caught 305 passes for 4,358 yards and 28 touchdowns, leading the team in catches in 1970 and 1973. After his career with the Falcons ended, Mitchell coached at two Atlanta-based colleges—Morehouse and Morris Brown—before becoming a volunteer assistant at the high school level in his hometown in Tennessee.

3. Andre Rison was known during his time in Atlanta for his mouth on the field as much as their production. Rison said he only talked smack—he called it "trappin'"—when

provoked, but it has sometimes caught up to him. Chris Hinton, Rison's teammate on both the Colts and Falcons, told *Sports Illustrated*, "Andre's mouth goes 120 miles per hour. In the huddle, it's a wonder any quarterback can get a word in edgewise. Andre says, 'I want the ball. Throw it to me. I can score.' Then, after the snap, I've got to hurry downfield to protect him from the other guys [opponents] he talks to." Rison also became known for his duck-walk touchdown celebration named "The Highlight Zone."

4. In the week leading up to Super Bowl XXXIII, Terance Mathis decided to reveal a very personal battle. Mathis admitted to having an alcohol problem and consulting with a doctor to help him deal with his alcoholism. Mathis did not enter any treatment center and did not quit alcohol, but he said he felt like he had won his battle with the disease.

5. The Falcons' trade for Peerless Price is generally regarded as one of the worst deals Atlanta has made in the last 20 years. In 2003, the Falcons sent their 1st round pick to Buffalo in exchange for the wide receiver, but the pairing never worked out. Price had thrived with the Bills, but he had just 109 catches for 1,413 yards and six touchdowns in two seasons with the Falcons before they released him in 2005. Atlanta had demoted Price on the depth chart before releasing him at the end of training camp as problems began to fester within Price's camp about the decision.

6. Alge Crumpler's biggest asset during his NFL career was his behind. Whenever teammates and coaches talked about Crumpler, his butt was bound to come up in conversation at some point. Crumpler was never a pass-catcher in college, but he became a reliable target for Atlanta's quarterbacks during his seven years in Atlanta. His butt played a large role because he could use it to box out defenders and give him more room to catch passes. As former North Carolina teammate Dauntae Finger quipped, "If it weren't for that (butt), Crump wouldn't catch a lot of passes. No one can get around him."

7. Roddy White blamed some of his own self-destructive habits for his slow start to his career in Atlanta. After coasting on his natural athleticism for much of his football career, his lack of film study and healthy habits caught up to him in Atlanta. In his first few seasons, it wasn't uncommon for him to drop passes or run the wrong route, all while taking advantage of Atlanta's nightlife scene. It got so bad that his mother came down to Atlanta after hearing that he was bankrupting himself, stole his credit cards, and had a heart-to-heart conversation with her son. White eventually turned around his career in 2007 after two mediocre seasons to become one of the best receivers in Falcons history.

8. Though he was not with the Falcons at the time of the incident, Tony Gonzalez saved the life of a San Francisco-area photographer in 2000. It was a simple football play as Gonzalez was hit out of bounds while playing for the

Kansas City Chiefs, and he ran over a photographer, Mickey Pfleger, knocking him unconscious. While conducting brain scans for a concussion at the hospital, doctors found a cancerous brain tumor on Pfleger's brain, and he had surgery in May 2001 to remove it. Pfleger died in 2010, but he and Gonzalez spoke on occasion throughout the decade following their original encounter.

9. There are too many stories about Julio Jones's athleticism to put in this book. He would play with logs and slabs of wood when he was younger, lifting pieces of wood that were roughly his size and just laying them on his chest. There are stories about how people around town knew Jones was destined for greatness from the third grade when the middle-school football coaches started to hear about him. He won the state championship in the triple jump with a 43-foot leap on his final attempt after fouling on the first two tries by using a far shorter approach than the rest of the competition. Then there was his dunk over Demarcus Cousins in a basketball playoff game during his senior year when he took off from the top of the key and slammed home a missed three-pointer.

10. When players were allowed to personalize their cleats for charity during the 2020 season, Calvin Ridley chose an organization close to his heart. He painted his cleats the sky blue of SOS Children's Villages in Florida, where Ridley resided as a child in the foster care system. After being drafted in the 1st round by the Falcons in 2018, Ridley went to visit the facility again and reflect on the

journey he had taken to the NFL. He entered foster care in the third grade with his two brothers, and one of the first things he told his social worker was that he wanted to be a professional football player, despite never having played the sport before.

CHAPTER 6:

TRENCH WARFARE

QUIZ TIME!

1. Which offensive lineman holds the Falcons' record for most career starts in an Atlanta uniform?

   a. Mike Kenn

   b. Todd McClure

   c. Jeff Van Note

   d. Bob Whitfield

2. Who was the Atlanta offensive lineman most recently named an Associated Press First Team All-Pro?

   a. Bill Fralic

   b. Chris Hinton

   c. Mike Kenn

   d. Alex Mack

3. Which offensive lineman held the record for most Pro Bowl appearances before Julio Jones broke it in 2019?

   a. George Kunz

   b. Bill Fralic

c. Mike Kenn

d. Jeff Van Note

4. Which member of the Falcons' starting offensive line in Super Bowl LI was drafted by the Falcons?

a. Andy Levitre

b. Ryan Schraeder

c. Chris Chester

d. Jake Matthews

5. Who was NOT one of the three Falcons offensive linemen named to the Pro Bowl in both 1981 and 1982?

a. Jeff Van Note

b. Mike Kenn

c. Bill Fralic

d. R.C. Thielemann

6. Atlanta drafted Jeff Van Note as a center when they picked him out of Kentucky in 1969.

a. True

b. False

7. Which of these Atlanta offensive linemen was NOT drafted in the top 10 by the Falcons?

a. Lincoln Kennedy

b. Bob Whitfield

c. Bill Fralic

d. Mike Kenn

8. How long is Jeff Van Note's record streak for most consecutive games played?

    a. 152

    b. 155

    c. 159

    d. 161

9. An undrafted free agent is the Falcons' all-time leader in tackles.

    a. True

    b. False

10. Which nickname did Jessie Tuggle earn during his career in Atlanta due to his bone-jarring tackles?

    a. The Hammer

    b. The Crusher

    c. The Mallet

    d. The Brick

11. Who holds the Falcons' record for most sacks in a single season, with 16.5?

    a. Vic Beasley Jr.

    b. John Zook

    c. John Abraham

    d. Claude Humphrey

12. Which team did Adrian Clayborn dismantle to set the Falcons' single-game sack record in 2017?

    a. New York Giants

    b. Carolina Panthers

c. Dallas Cowboys

d. Minnesota Vikings

13. Keith Brooking was the last Falcons defender to record 100 solo tackles in a season.

a. True

b. False

14. Who leads the Falcons with five fumble recoveries for touchdowns in his career?

a. Kenny Johnson

b. Tommy Nobis

c. Jessie Tuggle

d. Jonathan Babineaux

15. Who was the first Falcons player to be a First Team All-Pro honoree by the Associated Press?

a. Tommy Nobis

b. Rolland Lawrence

c. Claude Humphrey

d. Mike Tilleman

16. How many tackles did Tommy Nobis have as a rookie, which is still the team record for a season?

a. 273

b. 282

c. 289

d. 294

17. No Falcons player has ever been named the Associated Press Defensive Player of the Year.

    a. True
    b. False

18. Which of these Falcons defenders was NOT named the Associated Press Defensive Rookie of the Year?

    a. Al Richardson
    b. Buddy Curry
    c. DeAngelo Hall
    d. Claude Humphrey

19. How many sacks did Claude Humphrey finish with in his Falcons career to hold the franchise record?

    a. 92
    b. 94.5
    c. 96.5
    d. 99

20. Who blocked a Rams field goal in 1995 that Kevin Ross returned 83 yards for a touchdown to mark the first time a Falcons player scored on a blocked field goal?

    a. Pierce Holt
    b. Jumpy Geathers
    c. Lester Archambeau
    d. Roger Harper

QUIZ ANSWERS

1. A – Mike Kenn

2. B – Chris Hinton

3. D – Jeff Van Note

4. D – Jake Matthews

5. C – Bill Fralic

6. B – False

7. D – Mike Kenn

8. B – 155

9. A – True

10. A – The Hammer

11. C – John Abraham

12. C – Dallas Cowboys

13. B – False

14. C – Jessie Tuggle

15. A – Tommy Nobis

16. D – 294

17. A – True

18. C – DeAngelo Hall

19. B – 94.5

20. D – Roger Harper

DID YOU KNOW?

1. After Claude Humphrey was inducted into the Pro Football Hall of Fame in 2014, Lisa Kenn had an idea. The oldest daughter of Falcons tackle Mike Kenn started to campaign for her father to earn the same honor for his legendary career in Atlanta. Kenn holds the Falcons' record for most career starts and ranks second in seasons played with Atlanta. He was a three-time All-Pro offensive tackle and was named to five Pro Bowls. The campaigning worked because Kenn was a semifinalist for the Hall of Fame for the first time in 2015 and again earned the honor in 2016 and 2017. However, it is now up to the veteran's committee to enshrine him.

2. Jeff Van Note wasn't supposed to make the roster when Atlanta drafted him in 1969. He was a late-round pick and played primarily defensive end and running back at Kentucky, so his first time playing on the offensive line came during his rookie year with the Falcons. Ever the fast learner, though, Van Note took over as the team's starting center in 1970 and kept the spot for most of the next 15 years. He wound up making six Pro Bowls and was a Second Team All-Pro in 1982 while spending his entire career with the Falcons.

3. Bill Fralic was the leading voice within the NFL Players Association against steroid use and convinced then

NFLPA executive director Gene Upshaw to institute year-round random steroid testing in 1989. In May 1989, Fralic testified to the United States Senate Judiciary Committee about the use of steroids in NFL locker rooms and claimed at least 75% of all linemen, linebackers, and tight ends used some form of anabolic steroids. His testimony was called "refreshing and believable" by then-committee chairman Joe Biden, and Fralic became the face of the movement to clean up the sport.

4. Until Matt Ryan broke the streak in 2019, Todd McClure held the Falcons' record for most consecutive starts with 144 straight from 2001 until he missed the first two games of the 2011 season while recovering from a knee injury. He was a consistent presence on the Falcons' offensive line but never received any national recognition and never was selected to the Pro Bowl. That wasn't from a lack of effort from his teammates, however. In 2011, Tyson Clabo ordered red hats for everyone on the Falcons offensive line that said "McClure for Pro Bowl," including McClure's number 62. It was meant as a joke to rib the quiet leader, but Clabo also told reporters, "It's tongue-in-cheek, but it's also legitimate. Under his reign at center, we've sent multiple quarterbacks to the Pro Bowl, multiple running backs to the Pro Bowl, tight ends, receivers, other linemen. Well, he initiates every bit of it. I just think he gets overlooked a little bit."

5. Claude Humphrey's career almost ended in 1975 when he tore cartilage and ligaments in his knee. That was not an

injury many players could recover from in that era, but Humphrey was able to thrive after the surgery performed by Dr. James Funk, whom Humphrey credited in his Hall of Fame speech. The other doctor he credited in that speech was Charlie Harrison, who dealt with the blood clots Humphrey developed while being immobile after the reconstructive knee surgery. The life-saving procedure helped Humphrey return to the field in 1976 and set the team record with 15 sacks in that first season back.

6. Jessie Tuggle has proven that size doesn't matter at every stop along the way in his football career. Division I recruiters believed Tuggle was too small to compete at the highest level of college football, and many Division II schools felt the same way. The exception was Valdosta State, who used Tuggle as a defensive end his first two years before shifting him to inside linebacker, where "The Hammer" was born. His biggest break, though, came in 1986 when Mike Cavan became Valdosta State's coach for Tuggle's senior season. Coming from the University of Georgia, Cavan had connections with the Falcons that he used to get Tuggle a tryout in Atlanta after he went undrafted. Tuggle was able to impress the Falcons and prove that he could be just as devastating of a tackler at the professional level as he was in college despite being only 5 foot 11 and 230 pounds.

7. Keith Brooking led the Falcons in tackles for eight straight years from 2001 to 2008 but that didn't stop the front office from trying to look toward the future. The Falcons had

hoped Brooking would take on a lesser role with the team for the 2009 season, but the player believed he still had more good years left. So, after eight straight 100-tackle seasons, Brooking signed with Dallas as a free agent in 2009, and when the Cowboys played the Falcons, Brooking admitted to having a little extra motivation. "I would be lying to you if I were to say that I'm not trying to prove to these guys that I could still do it at a high level," Brooking said ahead of the 2009 matchup that Dallas won 37-21.

8. John Abraham decided to play football as a senior in high school as a way to win a competition with his girlfriend. He and his girlfriend were competing to see who could earn the most accolades in the yearbook, so he tried out for the football team, and after just one season, he earned a scholarship offer from his home state school, the University of South Carolina. After the Jets drafted him in the 1st round in 2000, Abraham was never comfortable in New York, so he ended up taking less money as a free agent to join the Falcons and be closer to his family and friends in South Carolina.

9. Vic Beasley went through a lot of turmoil in his life from his final season at Clemson through his entire first year with the Falcons. His brother died in a car accident shortly before that last year with the Tigers, and then his uncle, a close confidant of his, died during that senior year at Clemson. During his first year with Atlanta, Beasley spent much of the year visiting his dad in the hospital as he battled alcoholism and eventually died in April before

Beasley's second season with the Falcons. Beasley made up for it by leading the NFL with 15.5 sacks in 2016 as a second-year pass rusher but never again reached such heights in his career.

10. Grady Jarrett is making a name for himself with the Falcons, but he also has some strong bloodlines with the franchise. His biological father is Jessie Tuggle, and he considers Ray Lewis an uncle, though they are not biologically related. Tuggle was on the stage in Atlanta to help announce the Falcons' 5th round pick that they used to draft his son in 2015. Jarrett has a brother, Justin Tuggle, who played for the Texans and now plays in Canada.

CHAPTER 7:

NO AIR ZONE

QUIZ TIME!

1. Who holds the Falcons' record for most career interceptions?

   a. Ray Brown

   b. DeAngelo Hall

   c. Scott Case

   d. Rolland Lawrence

2. In which season did Scott Case set the Falcons' record with 10 interceptions?

   a. 1986

   b. 1987

   c. 1988

   d. 1989

3. The Falcons' record for most consecutive games with an interception is four.

   a. True

   b. False

4. Who is the only Falcons player with an interception return longer than 100 yards?

   a. Deion Jones
   b. Tom Pridemore
   c. Ken Reaves
   d. Ray Buchanan

5. Who is the only Atlanta player to return two interceptions for touchdowns in the same game?

   a. Ray Brown
   b. Deion Sanders
   c. Kevin Mathis
   d. Kenny Johnson

6. Atlanta set its franchise record for interceptions in a season in 1977 and matched it in 1980 with how many picks?

   a. 22
   b. 24
   c. 26
   d. 28

7. Who was the last Falcons defensive back to lead the team in tackles?

   a. Erik Coleman
   b. Marty Carter
   c. Ricardo Allen
   d. Keanu Neal

8. Ray Buchanan was the last Falcons defensive back to be named a First Team All-Pro.

   a. True
   b. False

9. Who was the last Falcons defensive back to be named to the Pro Bowl?

   a. Keanu Neal
   b. DeAngelo Hall
   c. Desmond Trufant
   d. Thomas DeCoud

10. Which of these Falcons defensive backs was a 1st round pick by Atlanta?

    a. Ray Brown
    b. Scott Case
    c. Bobby Butler
    d. Ken Reaves

11. Against which team did Bobby Riggle score the first defensive touchdown in Falcons history with a 62-yard pick six?

    a. Philadelphia Eagles
    b. Minnesota Vikings
    c. New York Giants
    d. Chicago Bears

12. Who has the most interceptions in Falcons history without returning one for a touchdown?

a. William Moore

b. Rolland Lawrence

c. Ken Reaves

d. Bobby Butler

13. What was Scott Case's legal first name?

a. Scotland

b. Scott

c. Jeffrey

d. Donald

14. Atlanta selected four defensive backs with its first pick of the draft between Deion Sanders in 1989 and DeAngelo Hall in 2004. Which one had the most interceptions for the Falcons?

a. Bryan Scott

b. Devin Bush Sr.

c. Michael Booker

d. Bruce Pickens

15. DeAngelo Hall scored as many touchdowns on fumble recoveries as a member of the Falcons as he did on interceptions.

a. True

b. False

16. Rolland Lawrence was an undrafted free agent pickup for the Falcons out of which current NAIA school?

a. Tabor College

b. Bethel College

c. Bethany College

d. Ottawa University

17. In which year was Rolland Lawrence named to his only Pro Bowl?

    a. 1974

    b. 1975

    c. 1976

    d. 1977

18. How many times did Deion Sanders make the Pro Bowl while with the Falcons?

    a. 0

    b. 1

    c. 2

    d. 3

19. How many passes did Deion Sanders intercept as a rookie with the Falcons in 1989?

    a. 7

    b. 4

    c. 6

    d. 5

20. Deion Sanders holds the Falcons' record for most interceptions returned for a touchdown.

    a. True

    b. False

QUIZ ANSWERS

1. D – Rolland Lawrence

2. C – 1988

3. A – True

4. B – Tom Pridemore

5. D – Kenny Johnson

6. C – 26

7. B – Marty Carter

8. B – False

9. A – Keanu Neal

10. C – Bobby Butler

11. B – Minnesota Vikings

12. A – William Moore

13. C – Jeffrey

14. C – Michael Booker

15. A – True

16. A – Tabor College

17. D – 1977

18. D – 3

19. D – 5

20. B – False

DID YOU KNOW?

1. Ken Reaves's tenure in Atlanta ended on a very sour note when he was traded in 1974. In eight years with the Falcons as one of the team's first draft picks, Reaves had 29 interceptions and became a leader on the team's defense. However, Reaves was also very active in the NFL Players Association and was a leader in the players strike in 1974. The day he helped start the first picket line outside the Falcons' facility, the team traded him to New Orleans. The NFLPA accused the Falcons of trading Reaves due to his union activity, but the Falcons said the trade had been in the works for months.

2. Ray Brown's career in Atlanta was overshadowed by the fact he was part of those early teams that weren't very good. However, he ranks second in interceptions and interception return yards in Falcons history. Though most fans might not know who Brown is, Archie Manning certainly remembers the hard-hitting safety. In 2014, a photo surfaced of Brown sacking Manning and turning him upside down with the hit.

3. Rolland Lawrence arrived in Atlanta as an undrafted free agent out of Tabor College in Kansas, having never played defense in college. He was a running back for Tabor and rushed for 1,076 yards on just 157 carries with 14 touchdowns as a junior. He wasn't as productive his

senior year against loaded boxes, but he came to the Falcons as a defensive back and let his skills shine. His only Pro Bowl appearance came in 1977 as part of the Grits Blitz defense when he had seven interceptions, two fewer than in 1975. He ended his eight years in Atlanta as the franchise's leader in interceptions with 39, a record that is not close to being touched in 2021.

4. While Tom Pridemore was starring on the field for the Atlanta Falcons, he was also representing his home state in the offseason. From 1980 to 1982, Pridemore was a member of the West Virginia House of Delegates representing Fayette County as a Democrat. He served just one term in the House and did not run for re-election in 1982.

5. Scott Case had several near-misses during his college recruiting process before he even made it onto the Falcons' radar. Coming out of high school, he almost signed with Oklahoma State, but Jimmy Johnson cut his scholarship money so he went to Northeastern Oklahoma A&M, where he won a national championship and was an All-American. He then almost transferred to Nebraska but never felt comfortable and ended up spending his last two years of college at Oklahoma. Case was drafted by Atlanta to replace Tom Pridemore at safety, but the two became really good friends and bonded over their love of hunting and fishing.

6. October 11 and 12, 1992, are dates that will go down in history for Deion Sanders and the two-sport athletes of the

future. In the span of a little more than 24 hours, Sanders played in two playoff baseball games as well as an NFL regular-season contest. On the 11th, he played the final three innings of the Braves' 6-4 win over Pittsburgh in Game 4 of the National League Championship Series. He then spent all night flying to Miami to play in the Falcons game against the Dolphins on the 12th. After the Falcons lost 21-17 to Miami, Sanders boarded a helicopter that took him to a private plane that flew him back to Pittsburgh, where he arrived in the Braves clubhouse minutes before the first pitch of Game 5. Sanders had three tackles and a nine-yard catch in the game against the Dolphins but did not appear in the 7-1 loss to the Pirates in Game 5.

7. Ray Buchanan had a musical talent that helped his cousin and him win various talent shows in high school. Buchanan joined the NFL Jams hip-hop record in 1997 and recorded several songs of his own, including "Hold On," which is still available on Spotify and most other music streaming services. Buchanan said his experiences on the NFL Jams record helped motivate him to record his own music, which he said was supposed to send a positive message to the children in Atlanta and the United States.

8. Like most rookies, DeAngelo Hall went through his share of hazing as a rookie despite being a top-10 pick for the Falcons in 2004. Because of his 1st round salary, the veterans on the team asked Hall to fund a team trip to Las Vegas. During that trip, the Falcons defensive backs

ended up at a nightclub with Paris Hilton and David Hasselhoff and racked up a $15,000 bill. Before Hall could even put his card down to pay the tab, though, Hilton swiped the receipt and covered the check for the team, saving Hall some precious money on his rookie contract.

9. Desmond Trufant had a lot of inspiration for his football career from his older brothers, Marcus and Isaiah, who are 10 and eight years older than Desmond, respectively. Desmond was always around the pair in high school, and their successes on the football field drove Desmond to play as well. Marcus wound up playing 10 years for the Seahawks, and Isaiah played 39 games for the Jets over four seasons while also playing for Cleveland and Philadelphia. Desmond Trufant credited the competition he faced as a child for his success early in his career after Atlanta drafted him in the 1st round of the 2013 Draft.

10. Keanu Neal had a fantastic start to his career over his first two seasons in the NFL with the Falcons. He had 106 tackles as a rookie and was named to the NFL's All-Rookie team in 2016, then followed up that performance with 116 tackles in 2017 and his first Pro Bowl nod. However, there were questions about Neal's durability entering 2020 after he tore his ACL in the 2018 season opener, then tore his Achilles in the third game of 2019. Neal said he felt like himself again entering the 2020 season, and he had a third 100-tackle season for the Falcons and also had a career-best nine tackles-for-loss and also came down with his second career interception.

CHAPTER 8:

SUPER BOWL SHOWDOWN

QUIZ TIME!

1. How long was Morten Andersen's field goal in the NFC Championship Game to send the Falcons to the Super Bowl for the first time?

   a. 38 yards

   b. 41 yards

   c. 44 yards

   d. 48 yards

2. Where was Super Bowl XXXIII played?

   a. Tampa Bay

   b. Pasadena

   c. Miami

   d. New Orleans

3. Atlanta never led in Super Bowl XXXIII.

   a. True

   b. False

4. Who scored the first touchdown for Atlanta in Super Bowl XXXIII?

   a. Jamal Anderson

   b. Terance Mathis

   c. Tim Dwight

   d. Chris Chandler

5. Who came up with the only takeaway of Super Bowl XXXIII for the Falcons by intercepting John Elway?

   a. Ray Buchanan

   b. Ronnie Bradford

   c. William White

   d. Cornelius Bennett

6. Who led the Falcons in receiving yards in Super Bowl XXXIII?

   a. Tim Dwight

   b. Tony Martin

   c. Jamal Anderson

   d. Terance Mathis

7. Jamal Anderson was the leading rusher in Super Bowl XXXIII.

   a. True

   b. False

8. How many interceptions did Chris Chandler throw in the Super Bowl XXXIII loss?

   a. 1

   b. 2

c. 3

d. 4

9. How many times were the Falcons penalized in Super Bowl XXXIII?

    a. 3

    b. 2

    c. 1

    d. 0

10. How many punts did the Broncos and Falcons combine for in Super Bowl XXXIII?

    a. 2

    b. 3

    c. 4

    d. 1

11. Who was the only NFC team to defeat the Falcons during the 1998 season?

    a. San Francisco 49ers

    b. Green Bay Packers

    c. New Orleans Saints

    d. Minnesota Vikings

12. How many consecutive games did Atlanta win after losing to the Jets before falling to Denver in the Super Bowl?

    a. 13

    b. 12

    c. 11

    d. 10

13. The Falcons were undefeated at home during the 1998 season.

   a. True
   b. False

14. Which single-season rushing record did Jamal Anderson NOT set during his historic 1998 season?

   a. Rushing touchdowns
   b. Yards per attempt
   c. Rushing yards
   d. Rushing attempts

15. Which team did the Falcons defeat in the divisional round of the 1998 playoffs?

   a. Green Bay Packers
   b. Arizona Cardinals
   c. Dallas Cowboys
   d. San Francisco 49ers

16. New England's only lead in Super Bowl LI came with the winning touchdown in overtime.

   a. True
   b. False

17. Who did NOT score one of the three second-quarter touchdowns that staked Atlanta to a 21-0 lead in Super Bowl LI?

   a. Devonta Freeman
   b. Robert Alford

c. Austin Hooper

d. Tevin Coleman

18. Who was responsible for three of Atlanta's five sacks of Tom Brady in Super Bowl LI?

a. Vic Beasley

b. Dwight Freeney

c. Courtney Upshaw

d. Grady Jarrett

19. Who was the Falcons' leading receiver in Super Bowl LI?

a. Julio Jones

b. Taylor Gabriel

c. Mohamed Sanu

d. Tevin Coleman

20. Which city hosted Super Bowl LI?

a. Minneapolis

b. Los Angeles

c. Houston

d. New Orleans

QUIZ ANSWERS

1. A – 38 yards

2. C – Miami

3. B – False

4. C – Tim Dwight

5. B – Ronnie Bradford

6. D – Terance Mathis

7. B – False

8. C – 3

9. D – 0

10. A – 2

11. A – San Francisco 49ers

12. C – 11

13. A – True

14. B – Yards per attempt

15. D – San Francisco 49ers

16. A – True

17. D – Tevin Coleman

18. D – Grady Jarrett

19. A – Julio Jones

20. C – Houston

DID YOU KNOW?

1. Jamal Anderson's 1998 season is still arguably the best single year ever for a Falcons running back. Anderson still holds the franchise record with 1,846 yards on a record 410 carries during the 1998 regular season. He went over 100 yards rushing a franchise-record 12 times, all of which came in the last 14 weeks of the season. He scored a touchdown in 11 of 16 games as well, and his 14 rushing touchdowns was a record at the time. Anderson ran for 113 yards and two touchdowns against San Francisco in the divisional round, but he was held to less than 100 yards in both the NFC Championship Game win over Minnesota and in Super Bowl XXXIII when he finished just four yards shy of the century mark.

2. It wasn't an all-time great season in Falcons history, but Chris Chandler had a career year in 1998 to lead Atlanta to the Super Bowl. It was his only 3,000-yard season, and he also set a career high with 25 passing touchdowns. He led the NFL in yards per attempt and yards per completion despite ranking 11th in passing yards that season. Chandler also missed two games that season, notably the loss to the Jets, but he showed up in the big games for the Falcons. The quarterback threw for 340 yards and three touchdowns in the NFC title game.

3. The Falcons had to overcome a little bit of adversity late in the 1998 season when coach Dan Reeves finally visited the doctor. After trying to push through to the end of the season, Reeves underwent quadruple bypass surgery and missed Weeks 15 and 16. Defensive coordinator Rich Brooks coached Atlanta to victories in those two games before Reeves returned for the season finale and coached the Falcons to the Super Bowl.

4. The 1999 NFC Championship Game will go down as one of the best games in Falcons history, given the situation and quality of the teams. Despite going 14-2 in the regular season, Atlanta was the number two seed behind 15-1 Minnesota, and the two teams met on January 17, 1999, at the Metrodome for a trip to the Super Bowl. Chris Chandler hit Terance Mathis for a 16-yard touchdown to cap off a 71-yard, 70-second drive for the game-tying score with 57 seconds left. Both defenses stood tall on the first possession of overtime, then the Falcons forced a punt from near midfield that pinned them at their own 9-yard line. Chandler completed all three of his passing attempts, including 15- and 26-yard completions to O.J. Santiago, to move the Falcons down the field, and Morten Andersen kicked a 38-yard field goal on third down to send Atlanta to its first Super Bowl.

5. Eugene Robinson was awarded the Bart Starr Award in 1998 as the NFL player who "best exemplifies outstanding character and leadership in the home, on the field, and in the community." Yet, on the night before Super Bowl

XXXIII, the Falcons safety was arrested for soliciting a prostitute for oral sex. He was released from jail and allowed to play in the game, but it was clear that the incident affected his performance. Robinson has not spoken much about the incident, but he did address the Carolina Panthers—for whom he worked as a radio analyst—before Super Bowl 50 about his mistakes.

6. Super Bowl XXXIII got off to an excellent start for the Falcons, who marched down the field for a 32-yard Morten Andersen field goal on the first drive. However, several key missed opportunities allowed Denver to pull away and take control of the game. After Ronnie Bradford intercepted John Elway deep in Broncos territory, Jamal Anderson was stuffed on fourth-and-short in field goal range. On the following drive, Andersen missed a 26-yard field goal, and Denver scored on the next play to take a 17-3 lead. The Falcons were never within a single score again.

7. The 1998 team still holds the franchise record with 14 regular-season wins and 16 total wins, and it set several other offensive records that were eclipsed by the 2016 Super Bowl team. The team also tied the franchise record with nine straight victories to close out the regular season. In 1998, the Falcons scored 442 points to break the record originally set in 1981, and then the 2016 team broke that record with 540 points. Atlanta scored 53 touchdowns in 1998, one more than in 1981, but the 2016 squad obliterated the record with 63 touchdowns.

8. The Falcons made the final game in the Georgia Dome a special one by defeating the Green Bay Packers 44-21 to reach the Super Bowl. Atlanta led 24-0 at halftime and extended the lead to 31-0 on the first drive of the third quarter. Matt Ryan threw four touchdown passes in the victory and added a touchdown run. Atlanta scored points on seven of their nine drives, with four of those drives covering at least 75 yards.

9. In addition to being the first Super Bowl to be decided in overtime, Super Bowl LI had a few record-breaking performances. Tom Brady set the record for most passing attempts (62) and completions (43) in a game as well as most passing yards (466), though he broke the yardage record the following year against Philadelphia. James White had 14 catches to set the Super Bowl record, and Atlanta's Grady Jarrett tied the record with three sacks of Brady in the Super Bowl.

10. Atlanta set a franchise record by coughing up a 28-3 lead in Super Bowl LI. After taking that large lead midway through the third quarter, the Falcons ran 16 plays for just 44 yards of total offense while New England scored on its final five drives to complete the comeback. The Falcons lost the coin toss and never saw the ball in overtime as Tom Brady completed five straight passes to march New England deep into Atlanta territory and then ended the game with a two-yard touchdown pass to James White, denying the Falcons' top-ranked offense a chance to respond.

CHAPTER 9:

SHINING THE BUSTS

QUIZ TIME!

1. How many future Hall-of-Famers have the Falcons drafted in their history?

    a. 2

    b. 3

    c. 4

    d. 5

2. How many players with ties to the Falcons organization are enshrined in the Hall of Fame?

    a. 7

    b. 8

    c. 9

    d. 10

3. How many times have the Falcons played in the annual Hall of Fame game?

    a. 1

    b. 2

c. 3

d. 4

4. Deion Sanders is the only Falcons player to have been a teammate of two different Hall-of-Famers while in Atlanta.

   a. True

   b. False

5. Who was the first player with ties to the Falcons to be inducted into the Hall of Fame?

   a. Eric Dickerson

   b. Tommy McDonald

   c. Claude Humphrey

   d. Deion Sanders

6. In which of his two seasons in Atlanta did Chris Doleman lead the Falcons in sacks?

   a. 1993

   b. 1994

   c. 1995

   d. 1996

7. How many games did Eric Dickerson play for the Falcons in 1993?

   a. 4

   b. 5

   c. 6

   d. 7

8. Tommy McDonald led the Falcons in receiving in his only season in Atlanta with how many catches?

a. 26

b. 31

c. 33

d. 37

9. Bobby Beathard served as Atlanta's general manager in 1971 before taking the job with the Dolphins.

a. True

b. False

10. Brett Favre made two appearances in his short career with the Falcons; which team was Atlanta playing when Favre attempted his only four career passes with the team?

a. Miami Dolphins

b. Tampa Bay Buccaneers

c. Los Angeles Rams

d. Washington Redskins

11. How many times did Brett Favre beat the Falcons in his five games against Atlanta during his career?

a. 2

b. 3

c. 4

d. 5

12. How long was Morten Andersen's kick in 1995 against San Francisco to set the franchise record for the longest field goal?

a. 59 yards

b. 60 yards

c. 61 yards

d. 62 yards

13. Morten Andersen is the Falcons' career scoring leader.

   a. True

   b. False

14. How many times was Claude Humphrey named to the Pro Bowl during his 10 seasons in Atlanta?

   a. 9

   b. 8

   c. 7

   d. 6

15. After suffering what many feared to be a career-ending knee injury in 1975, Claude Humphrey returned to the field in 1976 and finished with how many sacks?

   a. 12

   b. 13.5

   c. 15

   d. 16

16. How many games did Claude Humphrey play for Atlanta in 1978 before electing to retire for the first time?

   a. 1

   b. 2

   c. 3

   d. 4

17. In which season with the Falcons did Deion Sanders set his career high with seven interceptions?

a. 1990

b. 1991

c. 1992

d. 1993

18. Deion Sanders holds the Falcons' record with five combined punt and kickoff return touchdowns.

   a. True

   b. False

19. How many of Tony Gonzalez's 111 career touchdown catches came during his five seasons with the Falcons?

   a. 31

   b. 33

   c. 35

   d. 37

20. In which season did Tony Gonzalez finish with one more catch than Roddy White to lead the Falcons in receptions?

   a. 2012

   b. 2011

   c. 2010

   d. 2009

QUIZ ANSWERS

1. B – 3

2. C – 9

3. D – 4

4. A – True

5. B – Tommy McDonald

6. C – 1995

7. A – 4

8. C – 33

9. B – False

10. D – Washington Redskins

11. B – 3

12. A – 59 yards

13. B – False

14. D – 6

15. C – 15

16. D – 4

17. D – 1993

18. A – True

19. C – 35

20. A – 2012

DID YOU KNOW?

1. Claude Humphrey's exit from Atlanta put a damper on his great career with the Falcons. Four games into the 1978 season, Humphrey chose to retire after struggling to negotiate his next contract with the franchise. While on hiatus, he was a sports talk radio host in Atlanta and appeared on the popular television show, *The Dukes of Hazzard*. However, it was clear that he missed football, and his former coach in Atlanta, Marion Campbell, persuaded the Eagles to trade a pair of 4th round picks to the Falcons for the rights to Humphrey, who completed his Hall-of-Fame career in Philadelphia.

2. Deion Sanders made a joke about being bought on layaway by several NFL teams, but one of those teams wasn't supposed to be the Falcons. Only days before the season opener against the Rams did Sanders sign his rookie contract with the team. It almost backfired on Sanders when he muffed his first punt return of the season, but he fell on the fumble and was saved by a penalty on the Rams that forced a re-kick. On his second official punt return of the game, Sanders again dropped the kick, but this time, he was able to scoop it up on the run and dance 68 yards for the first touchdown of the game.

3. Morten Andersen's second stint with the Falcons was the end of a 20-month process for the kicker. He had finished

his 23rd NFL season with the Minnesota Vikings in 2004, and he continued training at parks in Atlanta waiting for the next phone call. The phone never rang in 2005, and it didn't at the beginning of the 2006 season, but Andersen kept grinding. He sat with a friend in his basement drinking beers while watching the Falcons play Tampa Bay in Week 2 of the 2006 season when he saw Michael Koenen continue to struggle for Atlanta. At that point, he turned to his friend and told him he was switching to water because his phone was going to ring. Later that day, his phone did ring, and he was at the Falcons' facility the next day for a tryout. In his Hall of Fame enshrinement speech, Andersen joked that his biggest decision that day was whether to sign his contract with blue or black ink.

4. Tony Gonzalez almost retired after Atlanta lost in the 2013 NFC Championship Game, but he returned the following year searching for one last shot at a Super Bowl. With Atlanta out of contention around the trade deadline in 2013, Gonzalez did not ask for a trade, but he certainly mentioned that he would be open to a trade to a contender. That 2013 season was a trying one for Gonzalez and the Falcons, and an ESPN article outlined his mindset as the season went along. The Falcons decided against trading Gonzalez because they wanted to retain his rights should he decide to return for the 2014 season. In the end, the 2013 season was the only one in which the Falcons did not have a winning record among the five Gonzalez played in Atlanta.

5. Bobby Beathard was a scout for the Falcons from 1968 to 1971 before he joined the Dolphins as the director of player personnel. Beathard returned to the Falcons briefly in 2002 as an advisor to owner Arthur Blank but decided to leave the position after just one year.

6. Chris Doleman is the only associate member of the Falcons' Hall of Fame contingent to play multiple seasons for Atlanta. In two years with the Falcons, Doleman had 16 sacks, forced two fumbles, recovered two fumbles, and had one interception. He was selected to the Pro Bowl in 1995 after recording 51 tackles, including nine sacks for the Falcons in his second and final year with the franchise.

7. In their second year as a franchise, the Falcons benefitted from their one season with Tommy McDonald at receiver. McDonald led Atlanta with 33 catches and 436 receiving yards in 1967, and he also was the team leader with four touchdown catches. McDonald had a catch in all 13 games in which he played, but his best performance might have been in Atlanta's only win of the season when he caught two touchdown passes, including a 41-yard bomb for the first score of the game.

8. Brett Favre only appeared in two games for Atlanta, and he did not show any of his Hall of Fame potential in those appearances. He made his debut against the Rams in Week 9 of the 1991 season but did not attempt a pass. He threw four passes two weeks later against Washington; two of them were intercepted, and the other two fell incomplete.

Andre Collins took one of Favre's interceptions to the end zone from 15 yards out to complete Washington's beatdown of Atlanta. Favre played against the Falcons five times after being traded by Atlanta and won three games while completing 67.5% of his passes, with eight touchdowns and six interceptions.

9. By the time Eric Dickerson arrived in Atlanta for the 1993 season, it was clear that the running back was a shell of his former self. He appeared in just four games for the Falcons that season, highlighted by his performance in Week 2 against the rival Saints when he rushed for 77 yards on 17 carries and had two receptions for 41 yards. The Falcons attempted to trade Dickerson to Green Bay in the middle of the 1993 season, but Dickerson failed his physical and then opted to retire.

10. The Falcons are eagerly awaiting a tenth member of the Hall of Fame with ties to the franchise, and two currently eligible candidates are close to induction. Linebacker Cornelius Bennett was a semifinalist for the first time in 2021, and Clay Matthews Jr. was a first-time finalist in 2021. The two linebackers barely overlapped in Atlanta, with Matthews starring from 1994 to 1996, and Bennett playing for the Falcons from 1996 to 1998.

CHAPTER 10:

DRAFT DAY

QUIZ TIME!

1. Which notable player was the first ever drafted by the Atlanta Falcons?

    a. Ken Reaves
    b. Claude Humphrey
    c. Randy Johnson
    d. Tommy Nobis

2. Which important contributor in their inaugural season was NOT chosen by the Falcons in the 1966 NFL Draft?

    a. Ken Reaves
    b. Junior Coffey
    c. Bob Riggle
    d. Randy Johnson

3. Atlanta's first three 1st round picks were all top-three selections.

    a. True
    b. False

4. How many times have the Falcons had the 1st overall pick?

    a. 6
    b. 5
    c. 4
    d. 3

5. Which of these Falcons legends was NOT a top-five pick in the NFL Draft?

    a. Steve Bartkowski
    b. Matt Ryan
    c. Bill Fralic
    d. Julio Jones

6. What was the first year in which Atlanta did NOT make a selection in the 1st round?

    a. 1967
    b. 1969
    c. 1971
    d. 1973

7. In 1969, the Falcons hit a home run when they drafted Jeff Van Note in which round?

    a. 8th
    b. 11th
    c. 12th
    d. 14th

8. Atlanta had two players besides Steve Bartkowski from the 1975 draft class play in at least 100 games for the Falcons.

a. True

b. False

9. With which pick in the 1st round did the Falcons draft Mike Kenn in 1978?

    a. 9th

    b. 11th

    c. 13th

    d. 16th

10. Atlanta drafted Gerald Riggs with which pick in the 1st round of the 1982 NFL Draft?

    a. 9th

    b. 12th

    c. 14th

    d. 17th

11. The Falcons drafted three players in the 1984 Supplemental Draft after the USFL folded. Who was NOT one of the players Atlanta picked?

    a. Joey Jones

    b. Scott Case

    c. Mike McInnis

    d. Dennis Woodberry

12. Who did Atlanta draft with its other 1st round selection in 1989 after using the 5th overall pick on Deion Sanders?

    a. Ralph Norwood

    b. Steve Broussard

    c. Shawn Collins

    d. Marcus Cotton

13. Brett Favre was the second player Atlanta drafted in the 1991 NFL Draft.

    a. True
    b. False

14. In which year did the Falcons spend a 4th round pick on a fullback from Utah named Jamal Anderson?

    a. 1997
    b. 1996
    c. 1995
    d. 1994

15. Which player did the Falcons draft with their 2nd round selection in 2001 after choosing Michael Vick with the first pick?

    a. Todd McClure
    b. Alge Crumpler
    c. Will Overstreet
    d. Roberto Garza

16. The Falcons used their first 1st round selection in 2004 to draft DeAngelo Hall, but who else did they pick that year?

    a. T.J. Duckett
    b. Jonathan Babineaux
    c. Matt Schaub
    d. Bryan Scott

17. From which school did the Falcons draft Roddy White in 2005?

a. Troy

b. Southern Mississippi

c. Louisiana Tech

d. Alabama-Birmingham

18. In which round was Atlanta able to snag Grady Jarrett during the 2015 NFL Draft?

a. 6th

b. 3rd

c. 4th

d. 5th

19. The last time Atlanta did NOT have a 1st round pick was in 2012.

a. True

b. False

20. With Atlanta earning the 4th overall pick in the 2021 NFL Draft, which player did the Falcons select the last time they held a top-five pick?

a. Matt Ryan

b. Julio Jones

c. Vic Beasley

d. Calvin Ridley

QUIZ ANSWERS

1. D – Tommy Nobis

2. B – Junior Coffey

3. A – True

4. C – 4

5. D – Julio Jones

6. A – 1967

7. B – 11th

8. A – True

9. C – 13th

10. A – 9th

11. B – Scott Case

12. C – Shawn Collins

13. B – False

14. D – 1994

15. B – Alge Crumpler

16. C – Matt Schaub

17. D – Alabama-Birmingham

18. D – 5th

19. A – True

20. A – Matt Ryan

DID YOU KNOW?

1. It wasn't a surprise when the Falcons made linebacker Tommy Nobis the franchise's first draft pick ever in 1966. The real question was whether they could sign the University of Texas product, who had also been drafted 1st overall by the Houston Oilers of the AFL. The Oilers reportedly offered Nobis more money, and an astronaut on the Gemini VII space mission even advocated for Nobis to stay home and play for Houston. However, Nobis said that he always wanted to play in the NFL and test himself against the best players, so he decided to sign with Atlanta.

2. There were a lot of scouts at Tennessee State to watch Claude Humphrey practice and play during his senior year in college. However, despite numerous promises from several NFL teams that they were going to draft Humphrey with their first pick, none of them ever had the chance. Instead, the Falcons selected him with the 3rd overall pick in 1968 despite never showing up at Tennessee State's practices like their NFL brethren. Humphrey admitted he was surprised when Atlanta chose him because the Falcons were not on his radar, but he respected the commitment the Falcons showed to him by drafting him that high.

3. In 1972, the Atlanta Falcons attempted to draft John Wayne, the 62-year-old actor, with their 17th round pick. Wayne, whose real name is Marion Morrison, played football at Southern California in the 1920s and had a modestly successful career before injuries ended it in college. There is film of Falcons coach Norm Van Brocklin asking the draft war room, "Do we want the roughest, toughest s.o.b. in the draft?" before submitting the name John Wayne out of Fort Apache State. Pete Rozelle disallowed the pick, but it would have been a story for the ages if Atlanta had held the Western star's rights.

4. When the Falcons decided to use a 3rd round pick on William Andrews in 1979, the front office could never imagine he would have the success he eventually had with the ball in his hands. At Auburn, Andrews was known as a physical blocking fullback and that was the role Atlanta envisioned for him when they drafted him. As the team's yearbook eloquently said during his rookie year, Andrews's "value is not reflected in rushing statistics, but devastating blocking ability." Yet in just five full seasons with the Falcons, he rushed for more than 5,700 yards and scored 29 touchdowns.

5. There was never a doubt that Deion Sanders wanted to be in Atlanta when he was coming out for the 1989 NFL Draft, and he did everything in his power to ensure that it would happen. He told every team that was picking before the Falcons at 5th overall that he was going to play baseball if they drafted him. He skipped out on meetings with the

Lions, who held the 3rd pick, to dissuade them from drafting him. He also walked out of a meeting with the Giants because they had the 10th pick, and he told them he wouldn't last that long. He had to work that hard because, on the field, Sanders was as impressive as they come after wowing the scouts with his time in the 40-yard dash at the NFL Combine, then leaving and not participating in any other drills. What stood out to Sanders about Atlanta was the number of black professionals in the city and how black people were thriving in the southern metropolis.

6. Brett Favre was a divisive quarterback when he was coming out of Southern Mississippi as a senior in 1991. Everyone knew he had hurt his hip in the East-West Shrine Game after his senior year, which came less than a year after he had 30 inches of intestines removed due to a car accident. The diagnosis from the doctors was avascular necrosis, the same hip condition that ended Bo Jackson's career. The problem with the condition is that it's impossible to tell how quickly the bone and joint will deteriorate from the lack of blood supply, so many teams decided to not take the risk on Favre. Others, like Atlanta, were willing to take the gamble on him and his talent, thinking his hip would hold up for six or seven years of good quarterback play.

7. The reaction from Falcons fans when the team drafted Roddy White in 2005 was mixed. He was a raw receiver who needed time to develop, and many fans would have preferred a player who could have made a more

immediate impact. Now that he is in the team's Ring of Honor, few fans would claim it was a bad selection, even if White's career in Atlanta got off to a slow start.

8. In hindsight, the Falcons were absolutely correct to draft Matt Ryan with the 3rd overall pick in 2008, but it was a selection that came with a little bit of contention as well. According to reports from Atlanta, the Falcons' scouts and general manager Rick McKay preferred defensive tackle Glenn Dorsey out of LSU to Ryan because McKay had questions about his arm strength and decision-making. Owner Arthur Blank preferred a franchise quarterback in the wake of the Michael Vick debacle the year before. Blank won out in the end, and Ryan ended up having a better career than Dorsey in the NFL.

9. The draft-day process was extremely stressful for Grady Jarrett on May 1, 2015. As he was watching teams pass over him in the 2nd and 3rd rounds, there was a major fire in his childhood home, burning all of his memorabilia and trophies from his high school and college career. Jarrett admitted that the fire only added to his emotions of that day because he was already disappointed about falling in the draft, and, at one point, he slammed his phone into the ground in frustration. He ended up watching the final four rounds from his cousin's house, where he got the call that the Falcons traded up for the first pick in the 5th round to draft him with the 137th overall selection.

10. Before he even arrived in Atlanta, Takkarist McKinley made some headlines for his emotional outburst after

being drafted in 2017 by the Falcons. In an interview on stage after Atlanta selected him with the 26th pick, McKinley was describing how much the moment meant to him while holding a framed picture of his grandmother, who raised him in Richmond, California, and died in 2011. He said he promised his grandmother before her death that he would play Division I football and get drafted into the NFL to escape Richmond. During the interview, he accidentally said a few curse words, but the NFL chose not to fine him for the profanity on live television.

CHAPTER 11:

LET'S MAKE A DEAL

QUIZ TIME!

1. The Falcons traded their 1st round pick in 1967 to the San Francisco 49ers in exchange for three players. Who was NOT one of the players the 49ers sent to Atlanta as part of the deal?

    a. Jim Norton

    b. Karl Rubke

    c. Jim Wilson

    d. Bernie Casey

2. From which team did the Falcons acquire Dave Hampton before the 1972 season?

    a. Minnesota Vikings

    b. Chicago Bears

    c. Detroit Lions

    d. Green Bay Packers

3. Which quarterback did the Falcons deal to the Lions as part of the trade to acquire Bob Lee?

a. Bob Berry

b. Pat Sullivan

c. Randy Johnson

d. Dick Shiner

4. The Falcons traded George Kunz to obtain the 1st overall pick in the 1975 NFL Draft.

a. True

b. False

5. Atlanta sent two draft picks to which team in 1985 for the 2nd overall pick?

a. Detroit Lions

b. Houston Oilers

c. Minnesota Vikings

d. Indianapolis Colts

6. What player did the Falcons draft with the 1st round pick they acquired from trading Gerald Riggs to Washington?

a. Deion Sanders

b. Mike Pritchard

c. Steve Broussard

d. Shawn Collins

7. The Falcons had to trade up to draft Deion Sanders in 1989.

a. True

b. False

8. Which other player did the Falcons acquire in 1990 when they traded the 1st overall pick in the draft to Indianapolis for a package that included Chris Hinton?

a. Mitchell Benson

b. Mike Rozier

c. Tim McKyer

d. Andre Rison

9. Which player did the Falcons draft with the draft pick they acquired in the Brett Favre trade?

a. Chuck Smith

b. Tony Smith

c. Lincoln Kennedy

d. Bob Whitfield

10. How many 1st round picks did the Falcons send to Indianapolis for Jeff George in 1994?

a. 0

b. 1

c. 2

d. 3

11. Both Chris Doleman and Jeff George were drafted by picks originally held by Atlanta that they traded to other teams.

a. True

b. False

12. What draft picks did Atlanta send to Houston in the trade to acquire Chris Chandler from the Oilers?

a. 1997 4th and 1997 7th

b. 1997 3rd and 1997 5th

c. 1997 3rd and 1997 6th

d. 1997 4th and 1997 6th

13. Which team originally held the 1ˢᵗ overall pick in the 2001 NFL Draft, then traded it to the Falcons, who drafted Michael Vick?

    a. Carolina Panthers
    b. San Diego Chargers
    c. Arizona Cardinals
    d. Cincinnati Bengals

14. Which wide receiver did the Falcons acquire in exchange for their 2003 1ˢᵗ round pick?

    a. Brian Finneran
    b. Trevor Gaylor
    c. Peerless Price
    d. Dez White

15. Which team traded 1ˢᵗ round picks with Atlanta in 2006, giving the Falcons the draft pick it sent to the Jets to acquire John Abraham?

    a. Denver Broncos
    b. Kansas City Chiefs
    c. Cleveland Browns
    d. New York Jets

16. In which year was the 1ˢᵗ round draft pick the Falcons acquired from the Texans in the Matt Schaub trade?

    a. 2006
    b. 2007
    c. 2008
    d. 2009

17. Which draft pick did the Falcons send to Kansas City in exchange for Tony Gonzalez?

    a. 2011 1st round pick
    b. 2010 1st round pick
    c. 2011 2nd round pick
    d. 2010 2nd round pick

18. How many draft picks did the Falcons surrender to the Browns in 2011 to acquire the draft pick they used to draft Julio Jones?

    a. 6
    b. 5
    c. 4
    d. 7

19. What did the Falcons do with the 2nd round pick they acquired from New England in the Mohammed Sanu trade?

    a. Drafted Marlon Davidson
    b. It was a 2021 selection.
    c. Traded for 2021 selection
    d. Traded for Hayden Hurst

20. Atlanta traded up for the 3rd overall pick in 2008 to draft Matt Ryan.

    a. True
    b. False

QUIZ ANSWERS

1. B – Karl Rubke

2. D – Green Bay Packers

3. A – Bob Berry

4. A – True

5. C – Minnesota Vikings

6. C – Steve Broussard

7. B – False

8. D – Andre Rison

9. B – Tony Smith

10. C – 2

11. A – True

12. D – 1997 4th and 1997 6th

13. B – San Diego Chargers

14. C – Peerless Price

15. A – Denver Broncos

16. B – 2007

17. D – 2010 2nd round pick

18. A – 6

19. D – Traded for Hayden Hurst

20. B – False

DID YOU KNOW?

1. The Falcons needed a return man entering the 1972 season, so Norm Van Brocklin shipped linebacker Malcolm Snider to the Packers for backup running back Dave Hampton. Van Brocklin was hopeful that Hampton's skills as a returner would help the team, but it was instead Hampton's rushing capabilities that stole the show. He rose up the depth chart to become the starter in Week 3 after coming off the bench and outperforming Joe Profit in the first two games of the season.

2. Entering the 1975 NFL Draft, the Falcons were still searching for their franchise quarterback. Fearful that their man would not fall to the 3rd overall pick, the Falcons sent their 1st round pick along with Pro Bowl tackle George Kunz to the Baltimore Colts for the first pick in the draft. Atlanta selected Steve Bartkowski with that pick, helping bring the franchise out of the doldrums of mediocrity.

3. One day before the Falcons traded Gerald Riggs to Washington on the second day of the draft in 1989, there were talks about a potential three-team deal that would have included the San Diego Chargers. Under the terms of that trade, the Falcons would have received the 8th overall pick in the draft from San Diego, which would have given Atlanta two picks in the top 10 that year. However, the Chargers pulled out of the deal and picked

Burt Grossman with the selection. The Falcons ended up receiving a 1990 1st round pick and a 2nd round selection in 1989 from Washington in exchange for Riggs.

4. In 1990, the Falcons held the 1st overall pick, and there was a hot race for quarterback Jeff George. Indianapolis ended up sending All-Pro tackle Chris Hinton, receiver Andre Rison, a 1991 1st round pick, and a 5th round selection in 1991 for that 1st overall selection as well as a 4th round pick in the 1990 Draft. George's agent, Leigh Steinberg, was ready to negotiate with Atlanta before the trade, but he flew to Indianapolis to quickly agree with the Colts, which was the last requirement of the trade. There was also a contingency if the pick the Colts sent to Atlanta in 1991 was in the top 12, but Indianapolis ended up with the 13th pick that year.

5. Four years later, Jeff George was disgruntled in Indianapolis, and the Falcons sent the 7th overall pick in 1994, a 1994 3rd round pick, and a 1995 2nd round selection to the Colts for George. That 1995 2nd round pick was upgraded to a 1st round pick when George started all 16 games for Atlanta in 1994. It was the second time that year the Falcons traded for a player who had been drafted by a different team holding a pick Atlanta traded to them. Atlanta acquired Chris Doleman earlier that offseason in a trade with Minnesota, nine years after the two teams swapped picks in the 1985 NFL Draft. The Falcons moved up to select Bill Fralic at 2nd overall, and the Vikings

settled for Doleman with the 4th overall selection acquired from Atlanta.

6. There are conflicting reports about Falcons coach Jerry Glanville's attitude toward Brett Favre after Atlanta drafted him in 1991. Many people around the organization claim that Glanville was very much against the pick, including general manager Ken Herock, but, in an interview with ESPN in 2016, Glanville said he was happy with the selection after the Falcons drafted a wide receiver in the 1st round. However, it was clear that Favre was not going to play in 1992 for the Falcons, so the Packers traded a 1st round pick in 1992 for Favre. Famously, Favre failed his physical with Green Bay due to his hip injury, but Packers general manager Ron Wolf overruled the medical personnel to finish the deal.

7. Chris Chandler came to Atlanta with a reputation for being injury-prone and a difficult person to have in the locker room. The Falcons had to surrender only 4th and 6th round picks for Chandler in 1997, and his teammates in Atlanta were skeptical when they heard the news. After the first workout, though, Jamal Anderson said the attitudes in the locker room changed toward Chandler, who would lead the Falcons to the Super Bowl in 1998.

8. The Michael Vick trade in 2001 was one of the few trades of draft picks that really worked out well for both teams. The Falcons traded a 5th overall pick, a 2001 3rd round selection, a 2002 2nd round pick, and Tim Dwight to the Chargers for

the 1st overall pick in the draft. The Falcons drafted Vick, who would become one of the most dynamic players in the league during his career in Atlanta, while the Chargers chose LaDainian Tomlinson with the 5th pick.

9. Atlanta's trade for Tony Gonzalez in the 2009 offseason was quick and painless after the debacle of six months before. The Falcons sent a 2nd round pick in 2009 to the Chiefs in exchange for Gonzalez, taking advantage of the greediness Kansas City had the previous October. The Chiefs had agreed in principle to trades with both Green Bay and Philadelphia for Gonzalez, but they raised the asking price in the final hours, and the deals fell through. Gonzalez was upset and threatened to retire and walk away on the spot, but he played out the rest of the season, then played five very productive seasons in Atlanta before officially retiring.

10. When a team homes in on a specific player, sometimes they are willing to offer a larger than necessary package to draft that prospect. That might have been the case for the Falcons in 2011 when they traded the 27th overall pick in 2011, a 2nd round pick in 2011, a 2011 4th round selection, and 2012 1st and 4th round picks to Cleveland for the 6th overall pick. It all paid off for the Falcons and general manager Thomas Dimitroff, though, as the player they targeted was Alabama wide receiver Julio Jones. By the end of 2021, Jones should hold all of the Falcons' major receiving records because he is remarkably close to Roddy White for the records he doesn't already hold.

CHAPTER 12:

WRITING THE RECORD BOOK

QUIZ TIME!

1. How many yards did Matt Ryan have against Carolina in 2016 to set the Falcons' record for passing yards in a game?

   a. 486

   b. 498

   c. 503

   d. 511

2. Matt Ryan has thrown for 5,000 yards in a season.

   a. True

   b. False

3. In which season did Matt Ryan most recently set the Falcons' record for most 300-yard passing games?

   a. 2019

   b. 2018

   c. 2017

   d. 2016

4. Whose franchise record did Matt Ryan tie when he threw for five touchdown passes against New Orleans in 2018?

   a. Chris Miller
   b. Steve Bartkowski
   c. Michael Vick
   d. Wade Wilson

5. Who is the Falcons' all-time leading rusher?

   a. Michael Turner
   b. Warrick Dunn
   c. William Andrews
   d. Gerald Riggs

6. No Falcons running back has ever had 40 or more rushing attempts in a game.

   a. True
   b. False

7. T.J. Duckett and Michael Turner share the single-game Falcons record with how many touchdown runs?

   a. 6
   b. 5
   c. 4
   d. 3

8. What is Michael Turner's record for most rushing yards in a game for the Falcons?

   a. 241
   b. 233

c. 227

d. 220

9. What is Julio Jones's franchise record for most catches in a season?

    a. 111

    b. 124

    c. 136

    d. 142

10. Who was the last Falcons player to tie the franchise record with three receiving touchdowns in a game?

    a. Julio Jones

    b. Terance Mathis

    c. Andre Rison

    d. Roddy White

11. How long was Roddy White's record streak of consecutive games with a reception?

    a. 127

    b. 128

    c. 131

    d. 133

12. In 2018, Julio Jones set a franchise record with 100 receiving yards in how many consecutive games?

    a. 4

    b. 5

    c. 6

    d. 7

13. Who holds the Falcons' record with five career interception returns for a touchdown?

    a. Rolland Lawrence
    b. Kevin Mathis
    c. Kenny Johnson
    d. Deion Jones

14. No Falcons player has ever intercepted 40 passes during his career in Atlanta.

    a. True
    b. False

15. Which two players share the Falcons' record of four straight games with an interception?

    a. D.J. Johnson and Ken Reaves
    b. Scott Case and Rolland Lawrence
    c. Robert Alford and Ken Reaves
    d. Ray Brown and Scott Case

16. Which Falcons linebacker holds the franchise record for most fumble recoveries in a career?

    a. Jessie Tuggle
    b. Tommy Nobis
    c. Keith Brooking
    d. Greg Brezina

17. Who holds the franchise record with 33 made field goals in a season?

    a. Matt Bryant
    b. Norm Johnson

c. Jay Feely

d. Morten Andersen

18. Morten Andersen became the first player in NFL history to make three 50-yard field goals in a game against New Orleans in 1995.

a. True

b. False

19. How long is the longest punt return in Falcons history, set by Deion Sanders in 1990 against the Bengals?

a. 77 yards

b. 79 yards

c. 81 yards

d. 82 yards

20. Who holds the Falcons' record for the highest punting average in a career?

a. John James

b. Dan Stryzinski

c. Matt Bosher

d. Michael Koenen

QUIZ ANSWERS

1. C – 503

2. B – False

3. A – 2019

4. D – Wade Wilson

5. D – Gerald Riggs

6. B – False

7. C – 4

8. D – 220

9. C – 136

10. B – Terance Mathis

11. B – 128

12. C – 6

13. D – Deion Jones

14. A – True

15. A – D.J. Johnson and Ken Reaves

16. D – Greg Brezina

17. A – Matt Bryant

18. A – True

19. B – 79 yards

20. C – Matt Bosher

DID YOU KNOW?

1. The Falcons opened the 1973 season with what still stands as the largest victory in franchise history. After a scoreless first quarter, the Falcons scored eight touchdowns and set a franchise record with 62 points as they blasted the Saints 62-7. The biggest loss in franchise history came three years later in 1976 in the second-to-last game of the season. The Falcons headed to Los Angeles to play the Rams and were blitzed 59-0, managing just 81 total yards of offense.

2. For Atlanta, 1983 was the year of the comeback. Both of the franchise's comebacks from 21 points down came during this season in which the Falcons finished 7-9. On October 23, the New York Jets had a 21-0 lead late in the third quarter before the Falcons stormed back with 27 unanswered points to earn a critical road game. Just over a month later, on November 27, the Packers scored the first 21 points of the game, but it was far from over. William Andrews caught a touchdown pass and then ran for a score to bring the Falcons within a touchdown. The teams then traded scores until the Falcons tied the game at 34 midway through the fourth quarter. The 47-41 overtime win over the Packers is just as famous for how the Falcons scored their final two touchdowns, as Kenny Johnson gave the Falcons their first lead with a 26-yard pick six, then won the game in overtime with a 31-yard pick six.

3. In his first game as a member of the Falcons, Michael Turner rewrote the record book in Atlanta. In the 2008 season opener against Detroit, Turner had 22 carries for a franchise-record 220 yards in Atlanta's win over the Lions. In becoming the second running back ever to rush for 200 yards in a game for Atlanta, Turner had a 66-yard rushing touchdown in the first quarter and capped off the quarter with a five-yard plunge. That second touchdown was preceded by a 29-yard run, the second of eight rushes of at least 10 yards in the win. Turner closed the season with a second 200-yard performance, becoming the first Falcons running back to rush for 200 yards twice.

4. October 2, 2016, was a record-breaking day for the Atlanta passing attack. In that 48-33 win over the Panthers, Matt Ryan set the franchise record by becoming the first Falcons quarterback to pass for 500 yards in a game. Ryan finished the day 28 of 37 for 503 yards and four touchdowns, with most of that yardage going to Julio Jones. Jones didn't come close to setting the franchise record with his 12 catches, but he obliterated his previous record for receiving yards with an even 300 against the Panthers that day. He caught just one of Ryan's four touchdowns, but there wasn't much else Carolina could do to stop him from breaking his old record by 41 yards.

5. In 2018, Julio Jones set the Falcons' record with 10 games of at least 100 receiving yards. Included in that was a record-breaking streak of six consecutive 100-yard performances. It began October 14 when Jones hauled in 10 passes for 144

yards against Tampa Bay, then continued with 104 yards against the Giants, 121 against Washington, 107 yards against Cleveland, 118 against Dallas, and 147 yards against the Saints. It was notably two notoriously difficult AFC North defenses that bookended the streak. Pittsburgh held Jones to just five catches and 62 yards on October 7, and Baltimore ended the streak with a dominant defensive masterclass by limiting Jones to two catches and 18 yards on December 2.

6. John Abraham was a nightmare for offenses to block in 2008 when he eclipsed the Falcons' record for sacks in a season by just half a sack. The year started strong with three sacks in the opener against the Lions, part of seven sacks in the first three weeks of the season. Despite finishing with 16.5 sacks, Abraham had sacks in just 10 games and had four multi-sack games, three of which were three-sack performances. Abraham set the Falcons' record in the second-to-last game of the season on the second-to-last play of the game when he sacked Minnesota's Tarvaris Jackson and forced a fumble.

7. Deion Jones doesn't intercept a lot of passes from his spot at middle linebacker, but when he gets his hands on a pass, there's a nearly 50% chance he's going to return it for six points. In just five seasons with the Falcons, Jones holds the record with five interception returns for a touchdown despite having just 11 career interceptions. In his third game as a pro in 2016, Jones sealed a big win over the Saints with a 90-yard pick six of Drew Brees. He

had a 33-yard pick six later that season to become the fifth player in franchise history to have two interception returns for a touchdown in the same season. He didn't score a touchdown in 2017 but had a 41-yard return in 2018, a 27-yard touchdown in 2019, and a 67-yard touchdown in 2020 to further extend his record.

8. In 10.5 seasons with the Falcons, Matt Bryant rewrote the Atlanta record book for kickers. He eclipsed Morten Andersen by scoring 1,163 points with the Falcons and twice set the single-season scoring record with 143 points in 2012, then 158 points in 2016. He holds Atlanta's record for consecutive PATs made with 257, as well as the Falcons' record for consecutive field goals made with 30. Bryant also holds most of the franchise's field goal records, including field goals made in a career (259), field goals made in a season (33), and career field goal percentage (88.7).

9. John James's strong leg set the Falcons' record for longest punt twice during his career with Atlanta. He booted a 72-yard punt in 1973 against the Saints and topped that with a 75-yard kick against the Raiders in 1975. The record lasted for 18 years before Harold Alexander tied it with a 75-yard punt in 1993 against the Bears. Two years later, Morton Andersen booted a 59-yard field goal to set the Falcons' record in the final seconds of the first half of a win against the 49ers. Matt Bryant tied that record in 2016 against the Chiefs on the final play of the first half.

10. No one played as many games for the Falcons as offensive linemen Mike Kenn and Jeff Van Note. Kenn holds the franchise record with 251 appearances, all of which were starts, and Van Note ranks second with 246 games played, including 225 starts. However, Van Note played 18 seasons in Atlanta, while Kenn put in "only" 17 years for the Falcons.

CONCLUSION

Congratulations on reaching the end of this exciting journey through the history of the Atlanta Falcons. We hope you have reached this point filled with new facts about your favorite NFL team. Whether you learned more about some of Atlanta's storied franchise records or were able to expand your knowledge with behind-the-scenes information about your favorite players and moments, we hope you enjoyed this trip through the rich history of the Falcons.

Being a sports fan in Atlanta is tough, and the Falcons' history certainly plays into that notion nationally. But there were some exciting moments along the way for the Falcons, and we tried to highlight as much of the positive as we did the negative in Atlanta's football history. It is sometimes easy to forget just how many great players have contributed to the Falcons and how many more great players will come in the future to wear the red and black. Claude Humphrey, Mike Kenn, and Deion Sanders are just three of the many notable names to have spent a significant part of their career with the Falcons, not to mention more recent icons like Jamal Anderson, Tony Gonzalez, and Roddy White.

We designed this book for you, the fans, to be able to embrace your favorite team and feel closer to them. Maybe you weren't familiar with the history of the franchise and the process of bringing professional football to Atlanta. Perhaps you didn't realize how well Atlanta has drafted for most of its history. Or maybe we just couldn't stump you at all, and you're the ultimate Falcons superfan. No matter how well you did on the quizzes, we hope we captured the spirit of the Atlanta Falcons and gave you even more pride in your team.

There is no doubt that the Falcons are in the middle of a rebuild entering the 2021 season, but one can never doubt Arthur Blank's desire to put a winning football team on the field for Falcons fans. There is a strong nucleus of players in Atlanta with a dynamic passing offense spearheaded by Matt Ryan with elite receivers Julio Jones and Calvin Ridley on his outside. The pieces are there for the Falcons to build their next title team, and it will be exciting to see how the new coaching staff and front office go about making Atlanta a Super Bowl contender yet again.